D1292101

VOICE

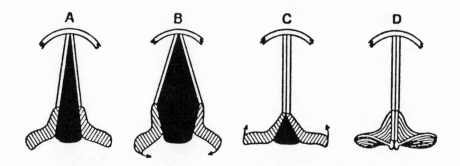

Position of the glottis during: (a) normal respiration; (b) heavy breathing; (c) whispering; (d) phonation. *Above,* the thyroid; *below,* the arytenoids. From Bertil Malmberg, *Phonetics* (New York: Dover Publications, Inc., 1963) p. 23. Used by permission of the publisher.

V̲OICE

DAVID A̱PPELBAUM

State University of New York Press

Published by
State University of New York Press, Albany

© 1990 State University of New York

For information, address State University of New York
Press, State University Plaza, Albany, N.Y., 12246

Library of Congress Cataloging-in-Publication Data

Appelbaum, David, 1942-
    Voice / David Appelbaum.
        p.   cm.
    Bibliography: p.
    Includes index.
    ISBN 0-7914-0287-8. — ISBN 0-7914-0288-6 (pbk.)
    1. Voice culture.   I. Title.
PN4162.A67   1990
805.5—dc20   89-35228
                                                        CIP

10 9 8 7 6 5 4 3 2 1

While the mate was getting the hammer, Ahab, without speaking, was slowly rubbing the gold piece against the skirts of his jacket, as if to heighten its luster, and without using any words was meanwhile lowly humming to himself, producing a sound so strangely muffled and inarticulate that it seemed the mechanical humming of the wheels of his vitality in him.

Herman Melville, Moby Dick

CONTENTS

PREFACE

The study of voice has a precise starting place. It is a place from which we are unexpectedly addressed by the sound of our own voice. In the dark woods, far from familiar signposts, we may, as we ask for directions, suddenly hear ourselves in that voice. The nakedness may act on us profoundly, opening us to a new direction. But the anxiety of losing one's way is not the only place of encounter. That place is both familiar and strange. Its location is anywhere. Exasperated, I tell someone to hurry up—and catch my impatient sound. Bored, I announce a change of plans—and hear my tedium. Happy, I declare a celebration—and notice my joy. In each instance, a recognition surprises me with its interrogation. Only the intensity differs as we move along the scale from the profound to the modest discovery. The shock returns us to the basic question concerning our most intimate acquaintance with voice. Whose voice is it, really?

The moment immediately opens another line of inquiry. For, in the night woods, we have gone merrily along conversing with companions before coming to the place where the voice is heard. We have not walked mutely along. Similarly, in my exasperation, boredom, or happiness, I delivered sermons, diatribes, and eulogies. Silence did not detain me. I am thrown into contact, immediate and undeniable, with the sound of myself in the midst of my voicings. In the place at which the study of voice begins, my voice is inescapably my own. No way around it exists. Yet until struck, I escape heeding the sound of myself in the voice. And after, I may deny the disturbing note as *my* own. That we avoid attending to the voice that is ours reveals a hiddenness surrounding voice. The hiddenness is double. The note of imperishable recognition is hidden from the being whose voice it is; *and,* we of voice lie in hiding from sounding the truth of ourselves. The twofold concealment provokes the second basic question: what enables us to avoid the profoundly or mildly disturbing encounter between ourselves and our voice?

The quest for the hiding place of voice provides me with a focus in the following study. We know from childhood games and mystery stories that things are best concealed when most in view. The most obvious occurrence of voice is in speech. Could our own voice escape discovery through our way of speaking with it? That speech covers over our unique manner of voicing ourselves is a radical suggestion. It indicates that the recovery of voice must lie in breaking the secreting power of speech—which does not mean, as the dark woods show, falling mute. The suggested inquiry, moreover, runs counter to a lengthy history of philosophy. History identifies spoken voice as the outer agent of thought in whose being resides judgment, truth, and knowledge. Thus, voice not modified and modulated by speaking, wild and woolly voice, supplies a crucial first test for hiding by speech. History claims that "crude," unspeechified voice is incapable of articulating truthfulness. Slurred, improper, curlish, animal, or demonic, such voicings that escape our lips unframed, themselves betray a lapse in or weakening of cognition. Since they lie outside the frame of speech, thought, and signification, how can they throw light on the subject of voice? Yet a cough or grunt, in its sounding, allows us to return to how we are in embarrassment or discontent. A laugh or the acoustics of the breath restores us to the place in which voice resounds in us. Unspoken and unspeakable voice recalls us from hiding to the grating joint of our reality. Hence my initial explorations ("The Cough," "The Laugh," and "On the Breath") attempt to uncover our own voice, voice's voice, from its hiding beyond the frame of speaking.

In the game of hide-and-seek, the one hidden freely relinquishes his or her place upon discovery. This fact testifies to the innocence of play. The hiddenness of our human condition behaves otherwise. The power of concealment is not surrendered upon discovery but contrarily takes active steps to erase what is brought to openness and to preclude further revelation. When we look again at the history of philosophy, this double action leaps to view. First, we find the erasure of voiced interruptions (squeals, rasps, gurgles, clicks, clacks, and wheezes) from the acknowledged interval of speaking. Second, we meet an increasing anxiety to retain control over the speaking voice and to defend against lapses in artriculated sound. Both occurrences lend support to my supposition that speech provides a hiding place for one's own voice. To what degree does intention enter into the act? The question of whether speaking is the knowing accomplice prompts me to investigate the elaborate apparatus of deception, retention, control, and authority which perpetuates concealment. This aspect moves the study through the middle chapters ("On the Verge of Madness," "The Metaphor of Voice," and "Babble"), further exposing the strategy by which voice is kept from self-recognition within the din of speaking. An elaborate means of concealing the loss of one's own voice emerges. Following Hobbes's analysis, I understand the means as inherently political insofar as their concern focuses on the exchange and barter of goods between persons.

If it occurs spontaneously (the child's game), hiding is innocence. If perpetuated and routinized, we encounter a technology of concealment. The technology that hides through speaking the loss of one's own voice is that of phonemic sound production. In mastering that technology, we lose the capacity acoustically to respond to a reality which repeatedly addresses us. On the balance sheet, however, the debit of one's own voice is offset by a technological gain: the deferment of the attention. Exchange by speech can take place without the demand of our attentive participation. The need to hear oneself as voiced is supplanted by the desire to communicate signs. The implications of a volition of absence occupy me also through the middle chapters, particularly in "Babble," and "Chant/Song." The theme is domination by the cognitive aspect of vocal experience over the kinaesthetic, proprioceptive one. The special vibratory, resonant quality of voice which awakens self-recognition is muted by the mind for signification. Even if voice appears from its hiding-place, the unattended ear is unavailable for hearing it. Thus does technology doubly secure recognition from encountering oneself in the voice.

One other theme interests me *vis à vis* the articulatory framing of voice by speaking. A look at the history of philosophy confirms the fact that the technology of deferred attention is compelled to speak of its own origin, though indirectly. This is a special case of the law that concealment must express its deed if only inadvertently. Both the means and the subject of expression are of considerable interest to me. Here we meet the venerable fable of the origin of speaking. Different philosophers have tried different versions. Hobbes's and Condillac's have a special force for me; Rousseau's and Diderot's, a lesser one. Each purports to show how speech came to be, and in so doing reveals the hidden act of secreting voice. The trace is peculiarly vivid in the metaphoric quality of the fable itself. The fable of the origin tells how an unspoken and unspeakable prototype is converted to a particle of speech. What is not and cannot be speech is rendered spoken by storytelling. The impossibility of such conversions juxtaposed with the fabulous accomplishment of the account leads me to seek in metaphor the clue to the action of hiding. This is the clue that I pursue through the chapters "How the Deaf Come to Speak" and "The Poem."

In the penultimate portion of the study, my concern is focussed on metaphor itself. Metaphor, being part of the sign system, obviously belongs to speech. Yet in the shock which momentarily strips us of speech, it holds the power to reveal ourselves vocally to ourselves. The metaphor returns hearing to the sound that we produce in which we resonantly respond to the world. The truth of the fable of origin lies in setting metaphor close to the unspeakable point. Its proximity to the act of concealment allows it to be truthful regarding its deception. The transparency of its concealment is given in the way it overtly conjoins speaking with our unvoiced, kinaesthetic experience. The authoritative posture of the technology of speech wavers as the play of human contradiction reappears at the margins of speaking. The force of contradiction alone provides the tonic against hiddenness.

The theme of metaphor leads me in the end to examine the poem whose speech is largely metaphoric. My last chapter, "Plato and the Poets," examines the act of metaphoric expression by assembling the various clues of Plato. Metaphor becomes the organic sounding of ideas, essences, or eternal objects through which we come to possess meaningful signs of our existence. Metaphor is primordial conjunction, adding acoustical value which "corresponds" to an unnamed element of experience. The nature of the correspondence is that mysterious act by which the unknown discoveries are allowed to fall out where they may. Rigor (but not rigidity!) pertains to one's commitments. In this regard I share with Derrida a primary commitment to the "law" of hiding: concealment cannot help revealing, however indirectly, its own action. One needs only to hold up what is spoken (the text) to this light in order to detect the lines of avoidance. As parallels converge on the horizon to the vanishing point, so avoidances gather at the hiding place. Uncovering that source of duality is a primary aim of study.

In commitment, strategy, and device, I am indebted to Derrida's work. Our agenda, however, differs markedly with respect to the origin, the vanishing point, and the place of concealment. Derrida is intent on showing that a study of the bipolarity reveals in the end that speaking is writing, and writing speaking. Both belong to that aspect of reality which can be signified—which is all that we can speak or read about. Whether the two are really fused or distinct is not paramount since the essential matter is intelligibility of the sign, word, or idea. His concern is, in short, to demonstrate the textuality of human experience insofar as it can be subject to philosophical study. The position is historically and currently sound. I noticed, however, that my initial reaction to Derrida's argument came with the watchword (borrowed from Rousseau, who borrowed from Aristotle, and cited repeatedly): *Voix*, not *sons*, are written. It struck me then and strikes me now that voice, on his analysis, becomes the audible sign; spoken voice, or the real, resonates in voice without loss. The voicing endures the way that presence does, waiting and durable. In this vein, I examine Plato's position in the *Republic* regarding the tragic poets. Their expulsion from the ideal political state has less to do with the control that they exert over the emotions than with their power to recall us to voice and voicing to ourselves. In their poem reside the buried vocal responses in which resound a recognition of the one whose voice it is. The danger that Plato ascribes to them concerns the recovery of deferred attention. His ascription is the work of irony. The poem's action is not to destroy the mind of signification but to remake it. Through the poem, we are recalled to the source of voicing. In its passage through us, voice gives audible expression to who we are.

In hiddenness is duality. I borrow that profound insight from Derrida. His exploration of the bipolar oppositions of speech, particularly in *Of Grammatology*, has furnished me with tools ample enough for the present study. The logic of reversal, substitution, and displacement derives from his work on these oppositions. My diverse applications of the logical transformations are makeshifts, strategic insights, and resourceful pratfalls. They do not constitute a method. Method itself is one pole of the opposition methodic/unmethodic, and so becomes slack, derigidified, labile, and unfixed under scrutiny. Method proceeds unmethodically. This is not to say that rigor is nonexistent, for a mode of procedure is essential in order for articulation of words. My first question was and is whether his confining voice to the outward expression of signs whose meaning derives from a system of signification is itself an act of concealment.

My sense is that Derrida's position hides the being of voice by limiting it to spoken recitation or the written transcript. For him, voice falls somewhere on the plane where lines of opposition run, whose page is apparently not ruptured by the advent of another level, hidden within signification like an unaddressed order of existence. Yet his own text intimates a fear of the place of concealment, the *coincidentia oppositorum*. Derrida recognizes that point as "where the fundamental signified is promised as the terminal-point of all references and conceals itself as that which would destroy at one blow the entire system of signs"[1] Add to this the fact that within the opposition speaking/listening, Derrida acknowledges nothing of the audible, acoustic dimension of vocal experience. All voicings could as easily be subvocal. These two discrepancies lead me to search for an approach to the voice which does not write over its authentically disturbing and inherently sonic note.

I take as a primary question concerning Derrida's thought the following: is the terminal or originary point at which signification abruptly collapses the moment when voice reveals itself resoundingly? An hypothesis follows from the query: that the shock of recognition—"Whose voice is this?"—liberates the kinaesthetic impulses to participate in and be interrogated by an unsignified and unsignifiable reality. I try various ways to examine my point. Corollary to my view is that we respond to the vibratory address by sensing the question of ourselves. Such voice *acts* on us immediately and inescapably. Interpretation and analysis—that is, engagement of voiced signification—are by second thought. This voice that escapes the written or spoken page is deeply organic and fraught with the problem of human suffering. From the midst of our cogitations, voice itself commends us to rediscover it. In all deference to Derrida's masterful exposition of hiding, when we encounter the sound that we sound as ourselves, we recognize that this voice remains concealed in his study. Perhaps necessarily so, given its potency and determination. With trepidation nevertheless, my intention is to investigate the prospect of freeing voice's voice and voice's body from the place of concealment, and to place it soundly before our ears.

CHAPTER 1

THE COUGH

Some say that the world ends with a bang. Others say a whimper. But a cough? For the villain hiding in the curtains, it is the end. The cough gives away the person. Edward, concealed from Lear, discovers as much. A whole universe may tilt with a cough. Alexander's did as the desert cough gripped his forces more tightly than the Persian army could. The cough is innocent flirtation or pompous oratory, a passing tickle made vocal, or the consumptive end of existence. It is not nothing.

The cough is the creature voiced. It is not the only way the human capacity for voice is exercised. The cough belongs to body and is of the earth. It is not pretty the way more foliate ramifications of human sound production are. Speech, song, the infant's cry, the wail of women, the idiot's babble, even the crowd's angry roar at the ballgame, claim more attention. These are the leaves and branches of a great and venerable tree. The cough remains with the trunk and below. It is not fit subject for discourse, poetry, or philosophy. In public one hides one's cough behind a hand or handkerchief. In private it escapes notice unless through annoyance or fear (illness?). Yet the cough has power. This power is not wholly that of its mute cousins, the shudder, the shiver, the tremor, or the shakes which also rouse one from sleep. Being voiced, the cough can waken recognition.

Born of Descartes's thoughtless matter, the cough sometimes excites a self-consciousness of its lowly origin. In itself the cough has no shame and does not lie—an early-found trait of voice. It is shameless like an eyeblink though both can be rendered devious through guile and rhetoric. Even if disingenuous the cough vocalically expresses the body, that is, the habitat, and perhaps a trace of its sometimes inhabitant, the person. Inanimate nature, volcanoes, cesspools, quagmires, mudholes, or the sea, may venture a cough. I have heard a mouse cough. Here, nature holds a mirror up to the art of the human body. Only the human cough, artful or otherwise, gives voice to an identity which is accompanied by the shadow or presence of a self-awareness.

The cough sometimes rises from the bowels, sometimes viscerally, sometimes from the manner of breathing itself. Always, air forcibly expelled from the lungs is made to work the voice box in its passage up and out. Even if delicate, the net effect is not as graceful as a well-executed utterance, a child's song, or a magisterial decree. The cough assaults the organ of voice. Is it, therefore, voice? The explosive noise has no less voice than the group of consonants known as voiceless. But its violence is different. A simulated cough still offends a sense of the voluntary which haunts the history of voice like a lisp. Is there volition enough in the spasmodic contraction underlying the cough to give it the good family name? Yet I have little difficulty recognizing my friend somewhere in a crowded theatre hall by his cough. To the oscilloscope, the cough is as reliable a mark of individuality as any voiceprint. The coughs of a man's life may be as numbered as his days and words, but are they similarly recorded? Some philosopher's prejudice is at work.

A life's first sound may be the cough, when the newborn's cry is throttled in the throat. A cough is the detonation of voice. It is duller than the pierce of a cry which goes to the heart. On the terminal ward, one hears the cries first. But the coughs penetrate more deeply, into the compact soma of the body. There they contact an organic memory which informs us of death and life as facts unembellished by feelings. If the world were cured of the common cough, we would be the less prepared for our earthly passage. Similarly while myth speaks of the gods' illnesses and maladies, nothing is told about their coughs.

Presumably their voices are not inflected with the mortality of an organic vessel. They do not cough because, even though subject to birth, they are incapable of knowing their own death. The same is true of angels who use their voices in human and celestial ways. To voice a philosophy without the cough is appropriate to incorporeal, supra-human beings. Perhaps, to philosophize so signifies a repulsion for the simple facts of organic life.

Voice has almost always been heard. People listen to oracles, song, practical command, and philosophical discourse. Assuming human production, the voice arises in roughly the same manner for everyone. Air moving along the chords of the voice box causes vibration like the river wind against a simple reed. Variable tension creates variations in the many qualities of vibration which are further controlled by throat, mouth, tongue, palate, teeth, and lips. The cough commonly makes its appearance as an interruption to the voicing process. It is not as pernicious as the stutter or stammer or chronic hiccup but nonetheless takes the attending audience with it. It distorts the text and texture of voice with the unexpectancy of the body. Thought has not always been a good listener to the pratfalls of the voice. Yet interruption has a history, itself interruptive as a playful cough. Aristotle is a way to begin listening to the neglect on which I want to dwell. On voice he pronounces that "what produces the impact must have soul in it and must be accompanied by an act of imagination, for voice is a sound *with a meaning*, and is not *merely* the result of any impact of the breath as in coughing." (*De Anima*, II.8.420b) The cough (at least the unpremeditated cough) is raw sound, unperiodic vibration, or plain noise. So much for the cough if voice is a mediated act requiring compromise and modulation of the body's language. Can one think the cough inarticulate? Consider the liar's guilty cough, the soliciter's embarassed one, the lawyer's cough to heighten dramatic effect, the lecturer's feigned cough to cover his misinformation, or Joseph McCarthy's nagging cough as the truth of the proceedings comes out. If a cough is a sound without meaning, how are we to understand Katherine Mansfield's poignant communication:

> The man in the room next to mine has the same complaint as I. When I wake in the night I hear him turning. And then he coughs. And after a silence I cough. And he coughs again. This goes on for a long time. Until I feel we are like two roosters calling each other at false dawns. From far-away hidden farms.[2]

The cough interrupts. The history of thought advocates against the body's expulsive punctuation mark. For the cough is not included. Yet the cough's puncture of vocal articulateness is as essential as the comma's or the apostrophe's, for voice must be phrased and phased to communicate. In the vernacular, the cough timid or brash is never absent for long. Only in refined, stylized deliveries is it erased, on the dramatic stage, for broadcasting, during public speeches, at the lecturer's podium, when the poet recites. The erasure reveals much. A history of erasure of the interruption speaks to a dogmatism and fear. Could the voice of philosophers be held in check by fear of the disruptive action of the cough and the basal regions of its bodily origin? Smooth, continuous, and unbroken, the voice seems to vocalize the sounds of angelic space, the Olympian heights, *nous*, the mind concentrated and cognitive. Throw in the lurching, grating, gyrating garble or gravel of the cough, and the presumption is hard to maintain. Unengineered voice is pregnant with coughs. In their hacking labor is born an unpretentious and therefore useful study of voice.

The news commentator's wretched cold plainly distracts listening from its customary channels. The story is lost in the repetitive history of the cough. Ending that history and starting a new one points out the editorial interest in the guarantees of voiced continuity and permanence. Eternity cannot be broken by cough. History has it that the soul, being a factor fixed and immutable, frequents this realm—with soulful sound, as Aristotle calls voice. Sound has soul only when embued with eternal meaning, meaning not distorted by cough-prone corpuscles. At just this point, the inquiry becomes pinched (as inquiry must) so as to keep out the philosophical dogs. Voice, sound, and meaning are so commingled as to make a natural unity. "Spoken words are the symbols of mental experience and written words are the symbols of spoken words." (*De Interpretatione*, 1.16a) One is naturally led away from the bodily interface with sound to a speech eliminating sensation. The erasure of the interruptive history that I speak of is the history of this "natural" guidance. Severe mental training is required to eradicate a cough as observation of a young child's interest in the same shows. Habit is second nature. The erasure, being habitual, takes on the aspect of a civilized virtue. The continual productivity of human discourse makes us forgetful of trained inadvertence. An unproductive cough may catch us up with it.

A good cough will rattle the shoulders and chest, making an unrattled voice impossible. But what if voice were primarily situated inside the head? "I mentally abused old Linton," speaks Nelly, of *Wuthering Heights*, to herself, "for (what was only natural partiality) the securing his estate to his own daughter, instead of his son's."[4] The natural history of voice inclines towards a kind of mentalization. Mental space is pristine, angelic, soulful, and unperturbed by bodily upheavals. It has been held interior, but this property is accidental to its meaningfulness. The essential is that unmouthed voice is stable enough to speak the tongue of eternal truth. The vulgar mouth lacks voice to do so if roguish, blaspheming, tongue-tied, inebriated, or prone to coughing. The mouth belongs to the appetites. It is vocally reliable only to the extent it is rote recitative. Aristotle's formula, "spoken words are the symbols of mental experience," doubly binds the voice. Only cognitive meaning cues grammar as to the matter of truth. Even if suppressed the cough is never mental and cannot be truthful. The cough, therefore, is to be feared. Its paroxysm is liable to upset the rarefied atmosphere in which the mind talks to itself. Self-speaking, inner vocalization, interior monologue: the entire history of soul-talk may be drowned out by a good cough.

The voice suffers with a cough, but remedies are plentiful. No patent medicines exist, however, to cure the voice of the possibility of a cough. That is fortunate since this despirited voice would lack its human root. A history of cough-free voice means a shift in the focus of listening. With the potential for cough-related destabilization eliminated, one listens to mental commentary. Clearer and more distinct in expression, refined voice has proof of existence on the tip of its tongue. Descartes needs to pay only lip service to the vulgar: "this proposition: I am, I exist, is necessarily true each time that I pronounce it, or that I mentally conceive it."[5] His disjunction is one of apposition. The organs of speech are, from the philosopher's point of view, vestigal. Voice cured of its susceptibility to organic maladies acquires the superhuman responsibility of speaking meaning and truth. The task allows no lapses nor margins of error for the body's weakness. Listening is drawn into the tight circle of the mind's speech, its experience, and the correspondence between the two. The attention is trained to defer to the symbol by which the two mind-elements communicate. This is difficult work. Small wonder that a cough makes the entire edifice shake!

The suppressed history of the cough is the story of narcosis. Narcotics suppress coughs. The tale is of philosophers' concentration of the attention in hopes of creating the Stone of the Philosophers. To concentrate means to separate into the usable and the unusable, the wheat and the chaff, the ore and the sludge, the distillant and the residue. Unfortunately, to purify the mind-order, the organs of speech have to be sacrificed. As such they are useless. Each age, since Aristotle and before, has had its officiates. At the earliest part of our own epoch, we find Locke, To conduct the cultural laryngectomy, Locke prepares the voice for a two-part operation. Though the net effect on the patient is the same as with earlier surgeons, the technique differs. Part one rigidifies, partially anaesthetizing the body's organs of voice: "Man, therefore, had by nature his organs so fashioned, as to be fit to frame articulate sounds, which we call words." (*Essay*, III.I.1)[6] Voice thus constricted speaks a natural phonetics. The invisible hand of nature plays the part that other epochs gave to God's name: to preclude the cough (and also the clack, the sneeze, the wheeze, and even the laugh) from the thesaurus of spoken voice. But why? If phonation must be articulate, why not the cough? It can be phonetically represented (as in a comic strip), alphabetically symbolized, and thereby separated into joints and segments. The story line demands that articulate voice serve a purpose higher than that of a spasmodic expulsion of sound. The voice is the heavenly messenger of words and the word is given voice through these organs. As Locke says, "for parrots, and several other birds, will be taught to make articular sounds distinct enough," yet parrots only mimic but do not exemplify voice. (*Essay*, p. 223.) Words, articulate sounds, dictionary meanings, and phonetic structure all get entangled with the will and higher destiny of man: the keeper of God's alphabet. The initial phase of Locke's operation makes man Egyptian and hierophantic.

The cough is devilish and chthonic. It interrupts God's sermon of phonetic abundance and the soul's self-reiteration. It dwarfs us as we bend double in its gutteral thrust. But most importantly it breaks our concentration on the delicate affair of framing the organs of speech to articulateness itself—which alone raises us above animal species. The second part of Locke's operation isolates the phonetic organ—the mind—and renders the physical organs of voice unneeded. The latter belong to an imperfect body the use of which is always a matter of necessity, never divine decree. Error, transgression, and falsehood stem from capitulating to physical need, that is, using the mouth and the rest as the instrument of voice. Locke says:

> Besides articulate sounds, therefore, it was further necessary that he should be able to use these sounds as signs of internal conceptions; and

to make them stand as marks for the ideas within his own mind, whereby they might be made known to others, and the thoughts of men's minds be conveyed from one to another. (*Essay*, p. 224.)

Propriety in speech is never vocal. It always is subvocal. Speaking is the sub rosa affair of concept and cognition. When we speak, properly speaking, we give voice to the mind's voice, the master's. Voice, moreover, suffers loss over the airwaves, due to the body's imperfection. Perhaps if the organs of voice did not serve two masters . . . Aristotle likewise notes that "the tongue is used both for tasting and for articulating." He goes on to conjecture that "in the case of the two functions tasting is necessary for the animal's existence (hence it is found more widely distributed), while articulate speech is a luxury subserving its possessor's well-being." (*De Anima* 420b) That thought, in Aristotle, degrades the body's functionings is an echo of Plato who says:

> The framers of us framed the mouth, as now arranged, having teeth and tongue and lips, with a view to the necessary and the good, contriving the way in for necessary purposes, the way out for the best purposes. For that is necessary which enters in and gives food to the body, but the river of speech, which flows out of a man and minsters to the intelligence, is the fairest and noblest of all streams. (*Timaeus*, 75d)[7]

That sound has to pass through the same orifice utilized by a lower, soul-contaminating function explains the accidental loss of propriety in spoken voice. Even though the cough fits the frame of the mouth perfectly, Plato reserves no Form for coughs. Locke's contribution to history makes mind-to-mind communication the only option for proper voice—unless it be writing. Locke does not take up the written word. Nonetheless, what is said against living voice is doubly true of the cough. It comes from the body and is sign for no God-given cognition. A bad cough has ruined many a prayer or meditation.

Voice rendered soft-spoken, *doce*, and sacred also renders truth. Doesn't Hobbes exclaim, "The first author of speech was God himself, that instructed Adam how to name such creatures as He presented to his sight"? (*Leviathan* IV)[8] Presumably, this is not the voice of the whirlwind which, calling our name, strikes with visceral impact. The divinity and divination of voice result from the high-minded operation of philosophers rather than the guiding hand of nature which Locke invokes. Nature strips us bare, leaving us exposed to ourselves. Voice then, should we cry out, is our own. Making voice fit to frame words, making voice mentally phonetic (and mind subvocally so), making voice immune to the cough, means leaving voice mute. Such is the explosive power of the cough, that truth seekers go so far to secure protection against it. For in terms of sound, the mute is the immutable. In a soundless universe, framing articulate sounds and listening to their high-fidelity reproduction need fear no disruption from below. Voice and the mind's ear now form a closed circuit. Meaning, the symbolic record of cognitive speech, is preserved from the shock of bodily presence. The interruption to voice has been erased in the name of truth. Truth is the ultimate cough syrup.

Erasure is never arbitrary. An erased history is the history of evasion from perceived danger, and fleeing for one's life is no plunge into random choice. Dreams, memories, and observations are made safe enough to become an ideal object by elision and inadvertence. Memory is imaged by what is deemed best not to remember. The stunning reversal of voice marks the escape route of a gadfly's victim. The victim, living voice, voice as vibrationally experienced, is chased to the ends of the civilized world, there to meet promethean technology. *Techne* or craft is the cunning mind reshaping nature so as to make it less shocking, anxiety-provoking, and overwhelming. The roadsign in the woods immediately reduces the infinite natural darkness to a matter of a few miles. Technology applied to voice leads to the amplification of the symbolizing "act of imagination" which Aristotle has stipulated. Technology hands the victor's laurel to the sign over the organically experienced impact of the body's sound production. Technology marks the final stage of conquest by the word, the unit of cognitive meaning, and its engine, the phoneme, the unit of sound discrimination. In the erasure, technology installs itself as nature, the new nature. The artificial and manmade is the natural. Locke notes the reversal, saying "words, which were by nature so well adapted to that purpose, come to be made use of by men as the signs of their ideas." (*Essay*, III, II)[9] Voice without technology, the voice of the infant, of pain, self-recognition, or passionate exclamation, or of bodily function (the cough), becomes inarticulate, ill-framed, "natural" babble. It attests to God's punishment for the human ego and its self-love as it came to pass in Babylon. Voice is redeemed and made good by the good will belonging to technology. "Words being voluntary signs" (Locke again) provide the means by which history reclaims the world from the abyss of nonsense—voice de-technologized and disconnected from its cognitive drive. (Ibid.) Without phonemics and grammar, the fundaments of technology, history would be meaningless balderdash—the cough.

The surgical removal of the organs of speech from voice stands exposed in light of a clear and present danger. The danger is madness but only in part. The jibberish cry of the madman is the lost mastery of technology. Frankenstein runs away from his inventor. His threat reminds us of the device which operates "naturally reconstituted" voice, technical meaning, truth, and divine assurance. The stranger's voice no longer strikes the chord of apprehension once we know his name. The device is the sign, the graphic desciptor representing interior subvocal words or the translation of sound into visual form. Such are words which

> in their primary or immediate signification, stand for nothing but *the ideas in the mind of him that uses them*, how imperfectly soever or carelessly those ideas are collected from the things which they are supposed to represent. (Ibid.)

The will in its arbitrary production of sound spells the ruin of voice remade and leads the speaker into madness. Madness is the passion of a private language, raised to dogmatics and immune to dialogue. It is intoxication with the power of meaning, which is the power of subvocal voice. Madness is the self-reference of rehabilitated voice made explicitly maddening. The history of voice has been told by thinkers who live in fear and trembling of insanity. But that danger is negligible compared to that of the cough. Madness is meaning, exponentially raised to self-reference. It thereby affirms the mentality of renatured voice. The cough is the body's interjection. It momentarily negates the mind's life. It shocks the cognitive apparatus in its brute reminder of organic experience. "The body, again, not remembered." While insanity hath method to its unreason, the cough is incommensurate. It is the null-space of articulate speech. It deranges far worse than the gap-toothed blitherer. From the yawning maw of its origin comes no word, nothing framed, yet sound. The body's cough erupts, rupturing the enclave's militated peace. The cognitive attention which had secured ("naturalized") the place is shocked to recognition of its incarnate condition. Momentarily, one's hold on the dichotomies of meaning-unmeaning, technological-barbaric, voluntary-involuntary, and mundane—sacred relaxes. One listens, not to words, signs, or symbols of mental events, for an entire notational system has been destablized. In the cough's ring, bark, or whoop sounds an unrelativized voice.

Being vociferous, the cough's assault on naturalized voice is absolute. In the recital hall, the speech does not begin until the coughs die down. The reason for the erasure of its rheumy history is that its interruption is unmediatable. The actor who in the midst of a Hamlet soliloquy cannot suppress it calls immediate attention to the technological supports of his speech. The profound beauty is, after all is said and done, only a theatre piece. The "involuntary" action of the actor's is more real. That the notational structure is so radically abolished reveals both the vocalness and the meekness of technological authority. Vocal because it almost always specifies the domain of voice as word, grammar, nature, and soul. Meek because it turns heel at the meekest cough. Even a cough rhetorically generated ("This is [cough] our finest hour") invites a new ear to history by its corporeal interjection. The audience is called to break with the past, continuity, soul-tradition, and unimpeded technological progress (the promethean myth), and to rise to the challenge voiced. The cough is of the cave, the black cavity of thorax and throat. Necessarily, it obtrudes on the mind's self-calmed quiet via the grimy mouth. The challenge is that bodily sound having no reckoning nor measurement defies a civil attentiveness. The promise is that somatic voice calls civilized man to a wider, freer awareness.

The cough is an attack on refinement of all sorts. Though one can cough cleanly (without inhibition), it itself is not clean. One hides a cough behind manners. The crude, unmannerly lack of soul denounces the curtailment of voice made mentally stable. The facade of symbol-symbolized, word-cognitive experience is touched on the raw. We are stunned that life goes on, though differently, when refinement is brought to a stop. The constant mental naming—God instructing Adam—refines by a reduplication. Locke says so: "words being sounds, can produce in us no other simple ideas than of those very sounds." (Essay, III.IV)[10] The cough cuts through the mental onomatopoetics to reveal our error. The error is not an error of cognition (mistaking one word for another) but cognition itself. Rectifying thought (let men "declare their meaning": Locke) perpetuates the inattendance. The only way to end the historical neglect of interruption is to interrupt it with the finality of a cough. Trying to reason is meeting the error on its ground—which is the idea of ground itself—on which the opposing position sounds like a meaningless barbarism. Can one risk sounding crude (the cough preceeding an expectoration)?

The cough as a return to voice: I have opened a study with a phenomenon of studied neglect. The suppression of a cough is an easy lesson at broadcasting school. Our ears learn even more quickly how to ride over the coughs punctuating the speaker's utterance. The audio tape of the same conversation surprises us with what was not listened to. In its continuous witness, the discontinuities of spoken voice appear bracketed by the staccato event of the cough. Technology is impartial enough to attest to what is erased in the name of technology (phonemics and grammar). Disruption emblazons the hand of mortality on human life. The double reversal of voice (its diminishment by refinement) must be understood in terms of a vocal preoccupation with immortality. Substituting inner speaking, the cognitive act, and the symbolic sound for the jarring vibration of the cough removes our direct acquaintance with organic processes. The corporeal intelligence knows directly of creaturely death with its power to interrupt life at any stroke. We return to knowledge in moments of immense threat or welcome. To train the attention to a mental focus then is to outsmart this knowledge—to outsmart death itself. The symbol is the manna which sustains, in a quite miraculous way, the immortal vision. Listening to the *vox naturalis*, one is kept safe from a death-inflicting confrontation with one's somatic mortality. Technology triumphs over nature in the moment-by-moment commentary that the mind provides. The more durable the representation, the more death is vouchsafed. The ultimate understanding of voice is not oral nor subvocal, is not vocal at all. Writing gives a transcription of voice, inner or outer, all of which conforms to Plato's dictum, "on the supposition that such writing will provide something reliable and permanent." (*Phaedrus* 275c)[11] The transcript is the graphic form of voice. The transcript is the quintessence of voice, the *vox vocalis*. To it, all vocalic tokens must be compared. The natural fallibility of voice (the cough) and the natural fallibility of the ear (distraction because of the cough) are replaced by the infallible written record. Lecture notes, court stenographs, microfiche, and (electronically) the displays of computer monitors partake of an eternity unavailable to spoken voice. The final solution of the double reversal of voice annihilates voice altogether. Even voice drawn inward fails to survive the transcript's power. The validity of mental speech, meditation, cogitation, and prayer is derivative and secondary. Strictly speaking, *speaking*, the natural voice of the soul, is found only in the silent act of reading. In rectification and elimination, Descartes affirms the transcript as the vehicle of truth: "the reading of good books is like a conversation with the best men of past centuries—in fact like a prepared conversation, in which they reveal only the best of their thought." (*Discourse* I)[12]

In the double metamorphosis of voice to cognition and cognition to reading, the cough is transformed by a hermetic act to nothingness. It never existed. The world is the text, the mind its reader. In order to learn all things, Descartes must only "read in the great book of Nature." Voice of any pitch or timbre is an echo of the page, having the same substantiality of Echo in the myth. Echo's unrequited love for Narcisssus, whose love is turned only toward himself, finally robs him of his body. Presumably, Echo cannot cough. Neither can the mind, narcissistically preoccupied with the Cartesian task of explaining its own states of affairs. In the world as text, the symbol stands for itself. The bodily rootedness which the cough exemplifies is forgotten. Cognition is decipherment, not of soul or world-soul for both are merely marks serialized on the textual page. The gutteral, gustational, respirational origination of voice is rubbed out. Sensation, tactility, the attention not mental but organic—in short, the incarnate position—has no place in the text. The double transformation reduces the stentorian dimension of the cough by a half, doubled. Fitting voice to the frame of the text is a case of amnesia. A kind of memory gets lopped off. Plato, who takes many contradictory sides on voice, cautions against textual propriety and the written word:

> If men learn this, it will implant forgetfulness in their souls; they will cease to exercise memory because they rely on that which is written, calling things to remembrance no longer from within themselves, but by means of external marks. What you have discovered is a recipe not for memory, but for reminder. (*Phaedrus* 275a)

Voice as soul-talk is less preferable than voice as reading. The antisepsis of graphic format kills the germs of coughs far better than cognitive monologue ever can. We fall asleep more easily over the printed page.

The cough keynotes an instrumentality of voice. Other instrumentalities are thereby disrupted. The nontechnological intervention against technology provides a clarion (or muffled if protocol partially intervenes) call *back*. To what? The question of specificity is lure of mind-stuff whose instrument eradicates all history of the cough. In the dark and mute woods, we simply follow the sound without question. The reverse flow traces the movement up and out from the pit of the throat, involving lungs, the organ of speech, and the mouth. The exit excites sensation. Sensation, so irritating in the cough that it maligns itself, invites contact. The somatic mass under contact is re-membered, put back together in alignment so as to vibrate sympathetically to the jarring nondiscursive sounding of the cough. Such is the act of memory, not of reminder. The organic intelligence harkens to the cough, not the textual reader ignoring it. Many acts follow memory, not the least of which is making past the interrupted interruption of history.

The history that I have traced devitalizes voice. From voice living and spoken to mental voice to technological voice, and finally to the written transcript, voice has successively been confined to more and more secure detention camps. At last inverted and rendered mute by the "invention" of writing, voice displays none of the vibratory energy which halts a progressive cognization of experience. "Our tongues are better suited to writing than speaking, and there is more pleasure in reading us than in listening to us," says Rousseau in the *Essay*.[13] Logos has become archival text, permanent, reliable, and bloodless. The transcript is subject to none of the vagaries of the embodied intelligence; its truth is *there* to be read. The textualization of life renders the standard of truth stable. The proposition, the highest invention of grammar, bears a truth-value. The soul whose truth once consisted in its harmony with the cosmos is contained in a graphic imprint. The truth of soul-talk depends on the action of the printed page: nonaction. This is the effect of propositionalizing truth. Locke confirms the fact: "truth properly belongs only to propositions: whereof there are two sorts, viz. mental and verbal; as there are two sorts of signs commonly made use of, viz. ideas and words." (*Essay* IV.V.2)[14] In fact the sign is unitary. Cognition and speech coincide like Spinoza's God and Nature. The essence of the sign is its legibility. Hence, "truth is the *marking down in words* the agreement or disagreement of ideas as it is." (*Essay* IV.V.8)[15] Human voice has lost its plasticity. It cannot reach across space with the booming resonance of an unrestrained cough. Its anemic vibration is subaudible, its space is the blank visual spacing between written words and it reaches no one's ears since it is dead to the airways.

CHAPTER 2

THE LAUGH

History begins and ends with the cough. The history of interruption begins and the interrupted history ends. In the cough the organism takes command (leaving aside the lecturer's cough-like sputterings.) Cognitive revision of voice—framing, articulation, inner monologue, cultivation of signification, loss of sound, the mute symbol—ceases, banished by the vigorous expulsion of vibrating air. Interrupted history is what Rousseau propounds in the formula, "Voice [*voix*], not sounds [*sons*], is written." (*Essay* 22) History gives a different sound to voice in the pause between breaths, before erasure. An intelligence speaks from out of the whirlwind of lungs and largynx, bronchial tubes and oral cavity. The cough takes the voice from us. What is its voice? The entire apparatus of distinction—natural/denatured, cultured/untampered, technological/pure, eternal/temporal—balances on the physician's spoon of expectorant. Can we say?

If we cannot, what about the laugh? The laugh is another agent of voice. Although it too begins in belly or bowels, the laugh is rich uncle to the cough. Because the laugh is of spirit, it has more upward mobility than the grovelling cough. One need not hide the laugh. Its spontaneity exudes charm, coyness, appreciation, wit, playfulness, and occasionally, an inner freedom. The laugh is not as free as the cough in escaping convention: heed the joke and its call for the auditor's responding laugh. Technology utilizes the laugh since it is more predictable than its poorer relation. We can "can" laughter. Also, more unpredictable as in the maniac's laugh (but not, cough). Having more spirit, the laugh enters history belligerently (the tyrant Nero's), trillingly (the woodland nymphs'), poetically (an orphic laugh), gustily (Falstaff's "Give me a cup of sack—I am a rogue if I drunk today"), or ironically (Socrates' satyric laugh). Far from being erased, one could tell a merry history by means of the laugh. Hence its value in telling the history of an interruption is more limited than the cough. The laugh does not ring as true.

How can it? The cough, being heavy and phlegmatic, stays low to the ground. The laugh rises to heaven, changing shape like an escaped balloon. Therein it betrays its pedigree. The laugh came into the world with trickery. The trickster lives in all but the most gentile laugh (and even there). Hermes gave Apollo a lyre that he had invented as compensation for a theft. Walking away scot-free, he laughed all the way home. Each laugh celebrates an act of thievery. All knowledge is stolen and through voice put to grammatical service. Saying "I am here" in the dark woods steals power from fear, allays it, but does not eradicate it. The unknowing is not thereby reduced since knowledge is strictly limited, and the unknowing, not. While the laugh is the noisy celebrant bursting into the symposium uninvited, the disruption is easily harnessed to the purpose of dialectic, argument, cognition, and soul-talk. Alcibiades' laugh blends in nicely with the erudite and intoxicated investiture of Eros which Socrates conducts. Alcibiades momentarily steals the attention with his laugh but his buffoonery is coopted by the refined voice of the general undertaking. The laugh at times covorts with its companion intoxicants. Which is another reason why the laugh disrupts history only mildly. The inebriant has poor memory, all is meaningful sign and portent, the wealth of signification anaesthetizes cognition—no sting of reality is felt. Yet the laugh, like the cough, owns the distruptive power. Descartes gives its fictional physiology of the cause:

> Laughter consists in the fact that the blood, which proceeds from the right orifice in the heart by the arterial vein, inflating the lungs suddenly and repeatedly, causes the air which they contain to be

constrained to pass out from them with an impetus by the windpipe, where it forms an inarticulate and explosive utterance . . . . And it is just this action of the face with this inarticulate and explosive voice that we call laughter. (*The Passions of the Soul*, II.CXXIV)[1]

Though fictional, Descartes's description has an accuracy that Spinoza lacks, who treats the laugh only by its cognitive redux, mirth. (*Ethics*, IV, Prop. xlii)[2] The laugh, when real, implodes established history. What do we really remember in the midst of a belly laugh? The body, convulsed or slightly shaken, is laughingly voiced. It is thereby shorn of articulateness and made fit for serving voice otherwise.

The laugh, therefore, does not embody a pure interruption. It is an intermediate joint between the cough and verbosity. Its affiliation with spirit gives it passion which always attracts cognition. With the laugh, thought is never far behind. Even the mocking laugh of the mockingbird seems to embody the reflective spirit. Thus we have pictographic and phonemic representations of laughter, unthinkable with the cough. "Laughing words—ha, ha!" reads the *I Ching*. "The shock terrifies for a hundred miles." (I.51; "Chen")[3] Phonemic representation lends greater technological value to the laugh. Its history is conceivable (the cough's is not) and one forthwith constructs a typology of laughter, e.g. the divine laugh, the devious-malicious laugh, the innocent (child's) laugh, and mad laugh.

Explanatory power impresses us. This exhibition of the laugh's expression dimension obscures its explosive aspect. How can a laugh say more than a thousand words? The laugh has eloquence and is therefore loquacious. Ahab's deafness to the portent of laugher is deafness to his mortal being, and Moby Dick's immortality: "Ahab did not hear his foreboding invocation, nor yet the low laugh from the hold, nor yet the presaging vibrations of the winds in the cordage, nor yet the hollow flap of the sails against the masts, as for a moment their hearts sank in."[4] Laughter was born already on the side of speech; if not already innocent, it must humble itself to remember its organic roots.

The guffaw no doubt disrupts one's mental concentration. But laughter can be so light as to be solely interior. T.S. Eliot describes the inner laugh:

> the leaves were full of children,
> Hidden excitedly, containing laughter.[5]

Nietzsche's Zarathustra, liberated from the spirit of gravity, "laughed in his heart and said mockingly, 'Happiness runs after me.' "[6] The inward laugh is probably closer to the mute laugh—the smile—than to the cough. The smile, as the French *sourire* knows, lives in silence underneath its vociferous kin. Both it and the inner laugh, having no audible shock value, are infinitely susceptible to signification, truth, and soul-talk. Yet to laugh, the plain truth is, is not to utter any word, any phonetically well-formed, "voluntary" sound-sign or phoneme. The contrary status of the laugh, its nontechnological meaningfulness, may lead one to imagine a language of gesture more primitive and natural than that of speech. Fictional history has the laugh come not long after the howl; I will speak at length of this below.

> The first language of mankind, the most universal and vivid, in a word the only language man needed, before he had occasion to exert his eloquence to persuade assembled multitudes, was the simple cry of nature. (Rousseau, *Discourse*, 176)[7]

Here is a signifying voice before the advent of the word! It must serve as origin and archetype for all human voice. Hence Aristotle's nomenclature for man, the animal which laughs, *homo ridens*. The conclusion inverts a series of inversions. Expression is inverted explosion, leaving the inner laugh more pregnant with meaning. Stability is inverted disruption, giving the mute laugh an eternal, soundless echo. Cognition is inverted corporeal impact, lending a syntax to laughter which is altogether lacking in real context. Othello's jealous laugh over Desdemona curdles blood. The ungrammared sound stops thought. It reverses the inversion and erasure of history. Without ceremony it graces the organic intelligence to remember the present and listen to the rumblings in the hold below.

Laughter is infectious but so is the cough. (I have sat, bored and impatient with a tardy lecturer, in a hall infected with sporadic fits of coughing.) The germ of dis-ease is freedom. Organically expelled sound blasts the attention from the tight orbit that it keeps by the laws of habit. The self-enclosed circuit of meaning, volition, and sound-signs is disturbed by a voice over which the ego has no control. To be free in oneself is initially to be free of oneself, the ego's grave voice. The volume and pitch of the laugh measures the momentary liberation from seriousness and self-concern. Thus "I hear all around me the most malicious, cheerful, and koboldish laughter," Nietzsche says,

> the spirits of my own book are attacking me, pull my ears, and call me back to order. "We can no longer stand it," they shout at me; "away, away with this raven-black music! Are we not surrounded by bright morning?"[8]

The laugh (the cough also) infects awareness with incarnate experience. Proprioceptive memory joggled, cognition temporarily cleared of obsessive soul-talk, we are available to the vaster vibratory vistas of an actual situation. The mute naming of creation no longer epitomizes human free will, as history has come down: "the mind, by its free choice, gives a connection to a certain number of ideas, which in nature have no more union with one another than others that it leaves out." (Locke, *Essay*, III.V)[9] The laugh reverses the terms of historically given freedom. It makes the name that I call myself (" 'I am', 'I exist', whenever I utter it or conceive it in my mind"), the *arche*-name, the butt of laughter. That a person is known in essence by such and such a name, is born, dies, is acclaimed, upbraided, cajoled, and vilified by a particular phonemic assemblage—and believes himself to be that name—is a joke of such magnitude that only a full-blooded laugh can explode it. It is a rare laugh, a catastrophic laugh, a laugh which ends death and life of the one who voices names. Thus:

> Yang Shan asked San Sheng, "What is your name?"
> Sheng said, "Hui Chi."
> Yang Shan said, "Hui Chi? That's me."
> Sheng said, "My name is Hui Jan."
> Yang Shan laughed aloud.[10]

Contagion must be transmitted, rendered outward before being taken inward. Of laughs and coughs, the acoustical part is infectious, the muted grammatical representation, not. Which is why the laugh seems independent of sane logic—and sanity. Both cold reason and tepid illogicality may be uproarious. Egocentrism and logos move around the same center, which is security from the unexpected and unreliable. Only conceited laughter (or the conceit of a well-placed cough) maintains the control of voice denatured, stabilized, and technological. hence precious laughter is noninfectious. In the madman's laugh, one fears infection in one's gut; in the malicious laugh, the fear attaches to the person who laughs. Divine laughter restores the fear and trembling to consequences unknowable and without reliability. Only the child's laugh has us forget the ego's eccentric flight; only then is the laugh voiced free from the syntactical constructions of ego. Only then do desire and suffering fail to resonate in voice.

In truth most any laugh comes with its web of syntax. This is both the danger of laughter and its promise which is greater than the cough's. Only the rare laugh destroys the text of ego. That could be the laugh to drive one mad. One latches on to the meaning-intention, the ensouled signification—and falls back into the orbit of the expressive. The deeply disturbing sound of the laugh, the fact of its incarnateness, its intimacy with the somatic processes of death and rebirth, its unique organic vibratory quality: the explosion of the laugh onto the world-stage becomes a tempest in a teapot. The intrigue of context carries cognition onward rather than arresting it on the spot. Aloysha, in *The Brothers Karamazov*, comes upon Mitya. "That's brandy," Mitya laughed. "I see your look: 'He's drinking again!' Distrust the apparition."[11] What kind of laugh is Mitya's? What does it mean? What is his motive? Grammatical investigations, definitive of character, preempt the arresting voice, the throaty sounding of wind against reed. Distrusting the apparition, our wish is to bury it in the elaboration of context. The pitch, modulation, tonality, tempo, and amplitude of the laugh, musically scored, are no less symbols of a grammar; they are less weighty, less grave, than those of speech. Music is closer to an unencumbered occurrence but still is a notational system, a technology. Rousseau realizes this:

> So long as one insists on considering sounds only in terms of the shock that they excite in our nerves, one will not attain the true principle of music, nor its power over men's hearts. The sounds of a melody do not affect us merely as sounds, but as signs of our affections, of our feelings. (*Essay* 60)

He reveals a cognitive repugnance for the incarnate position, conceiving "shock" in unintelligent terms: the twanging of a guitar string. How the organism is responsive to the shock of the laugh brings us to the abyss. The organic opening has the capacity to swallow cognition whole, and with it the apparition of the whole symbolized world.

Because the laugh is dubbed with ego (the cough, much less), it may shatter incompletely the notational framework of mental activity. Depending on how the ego attaches to history, the annihilation of context will bring freedom or madness. "Crazy wisdom" is a double annihilation. More likely the overlay will divert attention from the actual occasion, the peculiar modulatory flourish of voice that a laugh presents. The laugh is embedded in a study of its dramatic occurrence (in comedy), its everyday origination (the joke), its emotional machinery (humor), or the broad context in which the laugh is likely to appear (play). The laugh diverts us from itself. One tries to determine the logic of the laugh, its cause and explanation as though it were "a sound with a meaning," accompanied by "an act of imagination." The phonetic apparition ("Tee hee") is distrusted insofar as it is a real event. Thus the study has not yet attained escape velocity from the gravitational pull of the ego. The laugh remains theoretic, a twist of our rational nature. It signifies a dark, mute sign that only the soul knows within the closure of its domain. I can point to two instances where the laugh is explained rather than given voice to. Hobbes exemplifies the cognitive orbit in which the laugh falls spatially muted. He draws the simple equation, "the laugh" = "the pleasure of self-esteem":

> Sudden glory is the passion which maketh those grimaces called *laughter*; and is caused either by some sudden act of their own, that pleaseth them; or by the apprehension of some deformed thing in another, by comparison whereof they suddenly applaud themselves. And it is incident most to them that are conscious of the fewest abilities in themselves; who are forced to keep themselves in their own favor by observing the imperfections of other men. And therefore much laughter at the defects of other is a sign of pusillanimity. (*Leviathan* VI)[12]

Schopenhauer is even more intellectual in glossing the laugh. It "always signifies the sudden apprehension of an incongruity between such a concept and the real object thought through it, and hence between what is abstract and what is perceptive."[13] One wonders what becomes of the child's laugh or the madman's.

The laugh's double movement both interrupts and erases the interrupted history which the cough alerts one to. Who can heed the arrest and neutralize the grammar of soul-talk? Not Descartes, who full of promise, declares, "Experience also causes us to see that in all the possible occurrences which can produce this explosive laughter which proceeds from the lung, there is always some little element of hatred, or at least of wonder." (*Passions* II.CXXVI)[14] In the mind's eye, passion stands higher on the scale of understanding than the facts of embodiment. Is this because the emotions are more susceptible to transcription and to technical manipulation? The combinatorial science of rhetoric attempts to frame the voice of passion—"the modes of persuasion"—in order to show "why some speakers succeed through practice and other spontaneously" in reordering the cognitive experience of their auditors. (Aristotle, *Rhetoric*, I.1, 1354a) Rhetoric works on the arguments and theses of people because inner muted voice—voice made secure from the destabilizing effects of the cough and the laugh—is replete with feeling: cognized, intellectual versions of feeling. The soft voice of the soul is articulate with proper, quiet feelings. Necessarily, since Descartes warns "that the utility of all the passions consists alone in their fortifying and perpetuating in the soul thoughts which it is good it should preserve, and which without that might easily be effaced from it." (*Passions* II.LXXIV.364) Useful passion supplies cognition with drive. This makes possible technological stabilization. When Spinoza says, "Not to laugh, not to lament, not to detest, but to understand," he means the useful *versus* the disequilibrating.[16] And of embodiment? The raw, improper, brute sensation-producing coughs, sneezes, hiccups, belches, farts, and chest-rattles, having no true phonetic transcription, produce no soul-fortifying understanding. No rhetoric exists of the cough or the laugh. Concerning the gap in the mind's fabric of meaning, no meaningful technology of interruption exists.

The laugh explodes history with new voice: the Huns laughing outside the gates of Constantinople. The urbane voice is brought to a stop. The rigidified position of the jaw, the tensed operation of the muscular glottis, the tongue's ready poise: the frame of articulation relaxes momentarily in the primal cry. The savage laugh opens in a physical manifestation. Attila's demonstrative vocality is no event of the philosophical history which the laugh interrupts, the one of refinement, syntax, self-logic, and mutism. The body's living voice savages our technological hold on articulation. Nature's laugh can also stop us cold, like the hyena's in the jungle night. But it lacks the spirit of our friend's who laughs at a predicable lie. The savage laugh or every laugh not wholly contaminated by conceit ends the natural history of voice because it is immemorial. We remember that we do not remember the sound of our friend laughing. To remember is to be in the incarnate condition from which the laughing voice issues. We are left with an unexplainable impression—which explains why speaking voice tries to catch up with, eulogize, deprecate, annul, pacify, or commit genocide against the savage laugh.

By the same token, equating the laugh with the event of relief (like Nietzsche and Freud have) is like equating the sexual act with relief. No reduction serves vocalic force. True, the thunderclap or rolling sonic boom leaves semantics quivering in the wake. But the laugh is more than the discharge of a supercharged economy. It works release as a by-product of its quality of vocal remembrance. Relaxation is a result of the special action of voice, specifically, of the cessation of inadvertent tension associated with the cognitive function. To sustain the awareness of mental activity (the *sub voce* voice) takes a tight, cramped focus. The ordinary relation of voice to speaking is that of the arm holding up a heavy weight. It is contracted, taut, closed. The laugh works as headache remedy because it temporarily defocuses the mind. The harmonics and harmonization of the voiced laugh (and of living voice) are the other side of its destabilizing power; they require further attention and an attention which goes farther than the word-signs in cognitive activity. If the laugh spells relief, it is from the need to be relieved. In the act which recommences history, the register of voice operates outside the domain of relief—which is that of technology and control.

Only the rare laugh is unqualified by notation. Only rarely does one distrust Aloysha's apparition, so much less a part of the cough. The apparitional voice speaks with the meaning of a character. The sound fills a volume and is consumed in its articulation of the personality's purpose, design, desire, and passion. The laugh vibrates semiotically. One knows Heathcliff anywhere, in a crowded ballroom, across a field, or in the stable, by his laugh. The novelist, Bronte, exploits this fact: "Heathcliff having stared his son into an ague of confusion, uttered a scornful laugh."[17] The laugh is ready-made for a sentence. Purged is the laugh's power: to bring about violent revolution and overthrow the ego's dominion.

In the text of life, the laugh is not laughed. It is uttered, proclaimed, given, withheld, provided, or exchanged. As a token of speech, where is the horde's laugh, or Socrates' who (says Alcibiades) smites men "with a kind of sacred rage, worse than any Corybant, and my heart jumps into my mouth and the tears start into my eyes—oh, and not only me, but lots of other men"? (*Symposium* 215e)[18] To laugh meaningfully is to void a whole history of the inarticulate insurrection that the laugh instigates—or better, resurrection, because through the disruptive harmonics, the body is again raised, made sympathetically vibrant, no longer objectified by the scornfully cognitive look. The untranscripted laugh introjects intelligent life into the organism.

The laugh (along with the cough) is the beginning and the end of history. Either it carries along the momentum of a past which is present and obscures the present. Or it arrests the rush of thought, restoring the past to the past and allowing the elastic body of the present to form the moment. The laugh moves repetitiously across the web of meaning, signification, and monologue: why is there no beginning to the history of the interruption? We have already listened to Locke's insistence, "Words being voluntary signs, they cannot be voluntary signs imposed by him on things he knows not." (*Essay* III.2)[19] Voice-events must not overextend the domain carved out by intention. Outside that compound, one has no guarantee in the exercise of technological control. Barbarians laugh at the gate. To speak with them is impossible if communication supposes meaningful sound; one must turn to other means, e.g. the sword. The cognitive preserve of intention is modernized and defined by Husserl:

> Such sharing becomes a possibility if the auditor also understands the speaker's intentions. He does this inasmuch as he takes the speaker to be a person, who is not merely uttering sounds but speaking to him, who is accompanying those sounds with certain sense-giving acts, which the sounds reveal to the hearer, or whose sense they seek to communicate to him. What first makes mental commerce possible, and turns connected speech into discourse, lies in the correlation among the corresponding physical and mental experiences of communicating persons which is effected by the physical side of speech. (*Logical Investigations* I, sec. 7)[20]

Meaningful voice (the laugh) rests on shared intention, that is, of cutting voice down to the size of intention. intention infects the laugh (though it may not make it infectious). The laugh (voice) is not free until it is free from the germ of intention which continually revises history in order to unburden it of interruptions.

What is the force of the intention which pares human (and inhuman) sound-production from its meaning? A kind of refusal to heed, to listen, is involved. The question of meaning keeps us shut, the way it does when we are in a bizarre situation. When we are disturbed, to decipher is to hide from ourselves. Husserl shows this intellectual circumspection:

> A word only ceases to be a word when our interest stops at its sensory contour, when it becomes a mere sound-pattern. But when we live in the understanding of a word, it expresses something and the same thing, whether we address it to anyone or not.[21]

Obsessed by meaning, Husserl forgets an important kind of phonational experiment. A child will repeat a sound to cast its spell. Sufficient repetition provides the auditory counterpart of the prolonged visual gaze. A well-documented field-reversal occurs: in the shift from foreground to background, conventionally ("voluntarily") assigned meanings drop from objects. In the child's game of tongue twister (say "Black bug's blood" five times quickly), intentional signification likewise falls by the wayside, leaving a "mere sound-pattern," a quaint or ludicrous string of consonants and vowels, noise and music, voiced and voiceless sound. Even when transcripted into the phonetic alphabet ("blaablugsblah"), it corresponds to no filled place in the notational system. Hence, no meaning. Interest is not always so narrow, for instance, in the tongue-twister game or in the endless repetition of a sound-pattern called the *dharani*, found in yogic systems. In the first, attention to the sense of play leaves behind the field of intention and sign. In the second, attention to the absence of meaning works for a purpose which I want to study: to bring forth a voice not encumbered by conventions of sound production.

Husserl's idea thus announces a matter of great moment. Interest can stop short of securing meaningful human communication. When speaking together, our conscientiousness prevents us from appreciating the other workings of voice. As in debate, we keep cramping our mental wits for fear of losing our tongue. The fear is real. The child in a strange place knows that no food or drink is brought unless asked for. To keep a handle on one's speech is to prevent the decline of everything known and known to be good. Hence, Husserl's is principally a pragmatic and moral position.

The history brought to termination by the laugh (the cough) is a moral history. It is a history which questions Spinoza's precept to meditate on life, not death. These ultimate points have to do with the life and death of meaning and the subaltern intention, volition, and mental act serving the meaning. Thinking on death is moral since the fact of death offers the final (in some cases the only) test of one's moral thinking. The history of erasure and the erasure of that history, of the cough (the laugh), as propounded by Aristotle, Locke, Rousseau, and Husserl, is a history denying death. The death of the meaning-intention, its absence, its lack, is voided—and life, meaning, and mental focus made eternal—by the device of refusing the cough or laugh a phonemic address. This double reversal—organic disruption = death, cognitive fixity = life—serves history by moving oblivion beyond the enclave. Without the citadel of meaningfulness, one babbles or is mad. Hence we grow protective of what we mean. How to defend against the guerilla tactics of the subversive laugh (cough)? Yet the unexpectancy of coughing or laughing is given voice precisely in the death of meaning. Voice—without proper name or pronoun— forgets the forgetting and recollects a memory. The memory recalls the sounds which the organ of voice actually produces, their inarticulate frame, their lack of meaning, and the organic attitude toward the lack. In the wilderness of meaning, separated from the intention to signify, one remembers the powers of exile. In desert clarity, the reversals are obvious. We understand that the establishment of meaning makes the cough (the laugh) the pariah, the untouchable, and the outcast.

The history of which I speak is a moral one, in short, because of its fascination with the will to and life of meaning. Unsignifying voice exemplifies the death of volition. As Spinoza says, do not meditate on it. Unfortunately, the human habitat of will—the living, breathing body which contains the seed of willingness—lies beyond the pale of expressibility. Even the obvious gets left out. Meaningfulness "excludes (from expression) facial expression and the various gestures which involuntarily accompany speech without communicative intent." (Husserl I, sec. 5)[22] A tight circle is drawn around the points of intentional communication, volition, and meaning. That circle defines the mental attention. It contains the given, the *materia prima*, the bare substratum of all vocal activity. Puncture it with the unexpected bronchial tickle and the focus perishes. And with it, meaning. Husserl:

> In such manifestations one man communicates nothing to another: their utterance involves no intent to put certain "thoughts" on record expressively, whether for the man himself, in his solitary state, or for others. Such "expressions," in short, have properly speaking, *no meaning*. (Ibid.)

Husserl's desire is to banish the body's voicings (e.g., the cough, the laugh) from expressive meaning and have them wander in the desert of chance, involuntary, untoward organic interventions. The "accident" of human embodiment necessitates excommunication. Husserl's (and Aristotle's, Locke's and Rousseau's) is the desire for an angelic freedom from contingency, for a technology of thought (i.e. a universal philosophical language) whose control annuls disruption, arrest, violent shift, and the insurrection of life-forms vying with and against forces far surpassing their own mastery. This promethean fantasy would establish the human position higher than the gods, and set the mind's logos on a par with Jehovah's unreasoned will. It would mean final elevation of man's lowly origin, the triumph of the son over the father, the proof that willed destiny is stronger than fate. The distance to which this ambitious enterprise has been carried out philosophically testifies to its *moral* mission. Yet whenever vision turns to great heights, the small obstacle underfoot is often insurmountable. The voice muted in contemplation of divine thought trips over a simple syllable. The prayer is ruined. What voice is that of the renegade, the Jew? To this question I want to turn.

CHAPTER 3

ON THE BREATH

The initial impetus of an event is bipolar, whereas the history that follows is necessarily polarized and polemic. This is the case even when the account gives diverse viewpoints and embodies the principles of fairness and objectivity. The necessity shows that the record keepers have an ontological stake in the continuity of their chronicle. Otherwise their work passes from history into oblivion. The very idea of keeping a record, preserving a point of view, and maintaining a tradition is the strongest motivating force behind the kind of memory which invented writing. A memory predisposed to technology is happy, as Plato says, to barter recipes "not for memory, but for reminder." What is forgotten? Those moments of immense perplexity when we are unsure that our voice is our own. Then the univocity in vocalic history returns to origin and grows rank, ambivalent, many-voiced. Voice shows a most peculiar interruption which belongs only to a creature that breathes. Even before the cough and well before the laugh, the breath disrupts the continuous progress of voluntary phonemic production. More than other factors, we forget the breath.

This has not always been so. Aristotle says definitively: "in voice the breath in the windpipe is used as an instrument to knock with against the walls of the windpipe." (*De Anima* 420b) Here at the beginning of the history occurs an important and decisive elision. Human sound production *uses* the breath *as an instrument*. In this act of proto-technology, the voice maker reiterates the promethean theft of divine knowledge. Use of the breath in voice then becomes a primitive and primordial deployment of volition, eternally defining the breath in human experience. The breath as an unwilled, unintended organic phenomenon is annulled by Aristotle in proof of the *use* of the breath in voice technology. In voicing, respiration naturally ceases. Human voice grows celestial, without breath. Breath's instrumentality is confirmed by our inability to speak when breathing out or in—we can only do so by holding our breath; we make voiced movements only with the breath so checked. (*De Anima* 421a)

After this citation, critical to the history of voice, the unchecked breath is erased. Its role as interruption, spacing, arrest, and break in the continuity of voice production is replaced by musical or vocal scoring. Though the involuntary breath serves a memory which predates the interrupted history of voice, the breath does not remind one of the facts of the incarnate position. Just the opposite, since to remember the breathing while giving voice breaks the tight mental focus essential to speechification. We forget our train of thought. The history of voice that we are given is from this standpoint brief. It exists only so long as we hold the breath in check. It is thus the history of a peculiar practice: to stay the incessant rhythmic movement of the organism's life.

Erasure begins and ends by placing a check on the breath. History thus opens and closes. The history of voice that remains is one without breath—with breath erased—but with a check to delineate the outer limits of the enclave which vocal technology has secured. Beyond is the breath that we hear lost in the dark night of the woods: our own. Where voice is coeval with the check, its actual duration must be quite short, a matter of seconds, or with voice training, a minute or so. Then the involuntary takes over. One breathes, regardless of the will. The caesura of inhalation creates a need for renewed erasure. Spoken phraseology and the vocal in music camouflage the breath, relying on intonation, accent, the silence of rest, modulation of amplitude and frequency, and dramatic or emotional value. When the breath in speech or song obtrudes, the attention has been called to it because of vocalic or respiratory difficulty. Inadept technique, ignorance of the stops (being a novice in, say, French), or a wheezy throat makes one accutely aware of the breath and its obliterated history. Ordinarily the voice lives in the still-point of breath and the breath stirs in the muteness of voice. Voice is a proto-technological triumph of human signification over a vital intelligence. Which explains why the cough and the laugh belong only to a vocal prehistory: neither exercises a respiratory check. Which also explains why inner monologue is a final solution to the unreliable bodily-based voice. No such check is needed. The breath is dispelled from the mind's voice altogether. The mind does not perish like the breath. Therefore, mental voice is immortal.

No mere accident juxtaposes retention of the breath and the act *par excellence* of proto-technology, the voice properly prepared for speech. (Beware the cough or hiccup!) To reign in and hold onto the respiratory function provides the training ground for the ego's attention, the mental focus of cognition. Here lies the root of the mind's conquest of matter. Exercise in breath control is indispensable to the art of signifying, of denoting experiences through sound-images and words, the "voluntary signs." Imposing the will over the vital breath by setting it against the organic rhythm eventuates in the human capacity to know. Our rational nature comes into play by identifying a sign in relation to a signified and affirming or denying the relation. The sign is an acquisition of respirational conquest. Breath retention and articulate voice form two sides of the compound completed by knowledge and technology. Within the barbed wire lies all that humanity has won from nature. Voice without the breath check works for the guerilla forces against which articulation strug-gles. Under what banner are the enemy grouped? Noise, says Rousseau. "Whatever one does, noise alone does not speak to the spirit at all. The objects must speak in order to be understood. In all imitation, some form of discourse must substitute for the voice of nature." (*Essay*, 58) The end to noise is spoken voice, engineered by breath control. Precisely the quiet in which knowledge regroups to put signs on things and order in a world is what the held breath provides. Knowledge and technology, *episteme* and *techne*, share a common genesis. We may take the broad view that "both words are names for knowing in the widest sense."[1] In any event, each conept points to a program of pacification wherein the breath and the mind are simultaneously constrained. The program itself has a double value. Mastering the organs of speech by instrumenting respiration animates the cognitive function. It also eliminates the organic intelligence able to obey the unchecked breath.

Retention of the breath demarcates the bounds of voluntary sound-production. As Aristotle says, we make all movements of speech with the breath checked. Yet I know my breath so checked that I am literally beyond words. I cough and choke. Contact with the unretained breath—its dangerous potential for breaking, disrupting, or renting asunder the delicate mental focus—does not enter into the history of voice. After Aristotle, philosophy is wary of discussing the technology of voice and its cost. It publically emphasizes (for the purposes of diplomacy) the short eternity wherein self-will seizes control of an organic function and commandeers the vessel. The collapse of cognitive timelessness is endlessly postponed by the repetition of the same act of throttling—together with erasure of the lapsed interval of unregulated breathing. The spirit of erasure is visual. At least the lesson is learned from the eye and its relation to the mind's eye. The one blinks, the other "never sleeps." The mind's eye has no knowledge of the disruption to vision. The permanence of speech is the amnesia of its impermanence. Its fluent continuity is the self-will's expunging its string of broken failures. In the exacting measure of self-control, voice, the voice of meaning, the Cartesian ego, and the word (logos) live on.

History must necessarily take in new events. The philosophers' history of spoken voice is updated through the ages. The ethereal circle of willed voice, sound production, and retention is displaced, through the discoveries of modern physiology, to the muscular circle of the glottis. This advance is of great importance. It allows a consolidation of the secured space which respirational control has opened. The glottis is the laryngeal sphincter whose configuration comes under control of the intrinsic muscle surrounding it. Air pressure from the lungs passes through the glottis. The character of the air column causing the vocal cords to move rhythmically determines the production of sound. In the modern history of voice, the breath check becomes translated into a glottal stop. Exercise of strict retention is modified into a strictly controlled flow of the air. What we have is a primitive replacement. The zone of retention is widened and redefined without change in basic strategy: to silence the intrusion of noise. Control, "withal difficult, as proceeding from a watchful observation of the divers motions of the tongue, palate, lips, and other organs of speech," is simply recentered in the larynx. (*Leviathan*, IV)[2] Breath-control is supplemented by the tonus of the epiglottis. One is ever ready to produce spoken voice, even while dreaming. Descartes in his dream has voice enough to declare "the things that appear in sleep are like painted representations, which cannot have been formed except in the likeness of real objects." (*Meditations* I)[3]

The advance of decentralizing self-willed voice from lungs to glottis (from a pneumatology to a laryngotology) is one of super-imposition. The older form does not die off but is the refurbished part of the newer. Continuous voice regulation, the desideratum, is further buttressed. The cough, for instance, which poses the threat of severe breath depletion, now does only momentary violence. With enough control, a good speaker can almost talk through a cough. Glottal control, furthermore, overcomes the major weakness of the breath check: its necessary expiration. From a pneumatic standpoint, the desire of retention is self-defeating. Nature eventually wins out over human volition. Contingency bests logical necessity. No such countervoluntary rhythm intercedes with the glottis. Glottal control has the virtue of *at all times* a finger on the trigger. Voice production has been prized from the vagaries of the breath. The success can be tested against that gap in cognition which has never ceased to worry thinkers: sleep. Sleep-talk shows how the new technology connects the organs of speech to inner monologue. Word production in the dream in fact acquires a special status. It represents a wider realm of meaning and signification than met in glottal voice. The dream voice, I suggested before, lies closer to the eternal objects, the source of all meaningfulness. But dream voice is not a vocal (subvocal) alternative to the voice of cognition. Signs in the dream differ from cognitive ones without making a difference. The only difference is that dream voice, being even less perturbed by glottal insecurity, is closer to per-manence. Voice is no longer subservient to death's cousin, sleep. It lies at the cutting edge of new technology, dream signification. We may well be surprised at the conclusion: the dream provides the best verification of vocalic self-will. In the dream, one's voice is purest.

There is the matter of the whisper.

The whisper is further proof of the advance in vocal technology. It presents the critical experiment in the decentralizing and relocating of self-will. We need to review the Copernican hypothesis that forced a change in Aristotle's conception. The lungs are no longer the center of the vocalic universe. The voice box is. The rest remains the same. Voice still intervenes against interventions, the self-will defending itself against sneak attacks of its embodied condition. It still lives with the illusion of patching the broken seam of cognition. It still believes itself the echo of eternity. But the window of vulnerability left open by breath control is closed once and for all. In normal voice, the breath check restricts the air flow from the respiratory pump. With a breathy tone, restriction is less and air flow greater. The whisper, however, involves an almost nonexistent check on breathing. Air flow proceeds from the lungs as though there were no voice—yet there is the whisper! The whisper is the miracle spoken in the throat. With retention of the breath almost nil, volition manages to produce speechifying voice. Therefore, the seat of self-will is in the throat.

Thus vociferous history mutely erases all interruptions (the cough, the laugh, the sneeze, the belch) as unvoiced. It also records the implantation of an organ of speech—the technological *coup de grace* for *vox naturalis*. Inarticulate phonation is stripped of a power to sound thought-shattering alarm and disrupt the delicate operation of cognition. I speak of a shift in real power, the breath to the throat. The breath must expire. But the transplant allows thought and voice (i.e., voiced speech) to proceed *sans ârret*. Descartes the physician and student of human anatomy notices, "Our cognitions . . . which have the soul as their cause are cognisings of our volitions, and of all the imaginings and other thoughts which depend on them." (*Passions of the Soul* I.XIX)[4] The surgeon has grafted the soul onto the circle of the glottis. We sing his praise in that chief manifestation of soul, the attention.

Attention to spoken voice which required vigilance around the labile respiratory site can be deferred, derived, and made secondary:

> When in speaking we think only of what we wish to say, this makes us move the tongue and lips much more promptly and much more effectively than if we thought of all the various actions these must go through in pronouncing the words that express this meaning. The habits we have acquired in learning to speak have connected the action of the soul . . . with the meaning of the words that follow upon these movements, rather than with the movements themselves. (*Passions* I.XLIV)[5]

Meaning is the sequel to the will to voice (i.e., phonemic voice). Descartes obviates the respiratory pump altogether. Though nature abhors it, one could speak in a vacuum. Or the ether that the self-will breathes. The transfer of volition has an important vocalic spin-off. The semicontractile laryngeal muscles serve as a continuous reference point. Like division by a common denominator, they need not enter the account. Descartes' discovery that the body's movements can be cancelled is a more than the subtraction of a lack. It is the invention of a supreme device which does the subtracting. The gadget is the deferred attention. Deferred attention automatically suppresses respired voice anomalies (the cough, the laugh). "The great majority of our movements," Descartes continues,

> do not depend on the mind at all. Such are the beating of the heart, the digestion of our food, nutrition, respiration when we are asleep, and even walking, singing and similar acts when we are awake, if performed without the mind attending to them. (*Objections* IV)[6]

Descartes might have added two things. Voice, explicitly. And, that the mind's attendance does not weaken nor delete the automaticity of the movement, does not remove the lack but only replaces it with another from a different point of view. Respiration and voice are mechanically managed by the technology of voicification—whether or not one's mental focus is keenly fixed on the act. Such is the new autonomy of spoken voice. We catch a notion of it when a prerecorded voice surprises us in an empty room. Then we know that voice depends on neither respiration, the glottal masculature, nor the mind's guidance. It is a truly novel creation, disembodied and self-perpetuating!

Reviewing the steps to minimize the breath, one sees how far the phonemic approach has gone to bury the opposition. But any conquest retains the imprint of the vanished. Similarly no history obliterates the pattern of its origin. Take phonemic voice. The history begins with retention. To retain is to hold on to a presence in denial of an eventual absence. The trouble with respiratory retention is twofold. The retentive breath is still breathed. And the involuntary release of retention repeats the self-frustration of the strategy. Erasure must be repeated like clockwork to keep the lack in check. Like Prometheus's liver which is erased from existence by day, the need for inhalation grows back even in the night of retentive erasure. The breath check (Aristotle's invention) is a lack which must (by the laws of nature) be replenished. Retention is an absence which is a minus and must, with violence, be turned to a plus. But how does retention, as the will's strategem, begin? I think of the true origin of origins. The initial act of breath retention causes a downward pressure in the birth canal. Strangely, the held breath during child bearing, like the cough, the laugh, and the swallow, interrupts voice, understood as phonemic production. To vociferate while bearing down is impossible. Yet by transference the held breath fills the lungs with air and the air with voice. The first breath (an expiration) of the infant commemorates the pressure from the birth canal as it squeezes the thorax. The first breath necessitates the first voice, "the natural cry," nonphonemic and inarticulate, an inspiration in recoil of the compressed thorax. Thus breath retention (in childbearing) has a genesis that cancels, negates, and refills itself in order to give rise to the arche-act of voicing. An important corollary appears. Nonphonemic voice is the natural child of an unnatural, self-defeating will. Unarticulatable voice is born of necessity from the sickly anaerobic mother, the breath held in. Just as the postpartum mother takes deep breaths, the archetypal mother of voice perishes in childbirth. The occasion and ground of voice, retentiveness is always trying to better itself through good progeny. Voice, the good child, lives with the conscience of its mother's expiration. And this is the inheritance of voice—that it tries to be not itself but better: the vocal articulation of retentive meaning.

Each act and experience continually tries on its own birthing clothes. Voice is born in need. From need comes theft which is a great (but inhuman) invention. From the great need of voice comes the magnificent invention, the attention, stolen away, derived, deferred, and secondary. At childbirth, the voice is distinctly human. Who could confuse an infant's first voice with an animal's? As the infant lives out its vocal need, retentive meaning is imitated. Every child learns to speak the mother tongue. The seeds of cognition—the idea of the will and of the soul talking—are therein sown. Is not all learning imitation? Cognition is the mental embrace of theft, the attention stolen away, taken by the endless manipulation of signification, naming, speaking. The movement, as Descartes has said, is the more effective with the attention absented. The ending would be happy if we always remained in the condition of plenty. As with the retained breath, however, so with speaking voice: with the replacement comes loss. The loss is great, namely the specificity of *human* voice. So Descartes notices:

> I am well aware that beasts do many things better than we can. But I am not astonished at this. For this in itself serves to prove that they act naturally and by mechanisms, like a clock which regulates the hours, much better than we can by use of our judgment. And, beyond question, when the swallows come in the spring, they act in this regard like clocks. All that is done by the honey-bees is of the same nature. (Letter to Duke of Newcastle, November 1646)[7]

Effectiveness in voice, its capacity to mimic retentive meaning, the mother tongue, involves the economy of theft. But theft is a poor economy. Taking from is always a being taken from. The thief takes from his prey (Hermes from Apollo) and at the same time has the inventions (the lyre) taken from him. Voice takes the phoneme and the mechanism of phonetic reproduction, the deferred attention together with the glottal membrane. It thereby relinquishes the vocalic memory. A recollection which is specifically human and able to respond with the specifically human vocation of voice is thereby taken from us. This memory is not to be retained nor grasped nor possessed. Its sounds may or may not express meaning. If expressive, they may be so incidently or essentially. The specificity of the voice of remembrance is not entirely forgotten by Descartes, who nonetheless crosses the nerves to it in order to perserve the crossed history:

> Besides the corporeal memory whose impressions can be explained by the cerebral traces, I hold that in our understanding we have yet another sort of memory, which is entirely spiritual, and not to be found in the beasts. (Letter to Mersenne, August 6, 1640)[8]

The voice of remembrance, however, does not resonate in the mind or soul, for Hermetic memory is theft, imitation, the deferring of attention. Such voice as shocks the soul into an unmediated, non-phonemic, designifying recognition of the specifically human is the broken, gap-toothed, violent, guerilla sound of the corporeal mass. That sound imitates nothing. Its attention is undeferred since it stands in deference to nothing. In the unequal, irresolvable confrontation of the retentive mother tongue of voice, and voice incarnate, neither is taken up by the other (though speech would have it so). Frictive, abrasive, uneloquent, such voices burst from its organic fold—the voicebox—to resurrect the specifically human in the mechanically arranged world.

I recapitulate a history of voice which began with Aristotle saying, "the breath in the windpipe is used as an instrument to knock with against the walls of the windpipe." A single note quickly established itself as the voice of history. The technology of breath therein subjugates forever the respiratory function to the means of producing phonemic voice. The by-product is the more important invention: an attention derived, delayed, made habitual, and awaiting the moment of being immediate and attentive—which may never arise. Secondary attention is decentered and displaced to the largyx, with a corresponding shift in soul- and signification-making powers.

Though the operation is not completed until modern times, Aristotle lays provisions: "Voice then is the impact of the inbreathed air against the 'windpipe', and the agent that produces the impact is the soul resident in these parts of the body." (*De Anima* 420b) The operation has magical effects since magic always jars with the innocence of its causality. I have already looked at this in a slightly different context. To place the breath in deference to phonemics is to cast a spell of amnesia over voice. An order is inverted. Pneumatics is erased in favor of logic. Validity takes on the economy of efficiency. Making voice becomes audible reading because phonemic voice is most effective in its ability to *read* writing (Plato), "to rely on that which is written . . . by means of external marks." (*Phaedrus* 275a) The mutating of human sound, with the specific gravity of its vibration, is effected by habituated self-will reading the mind's script *via* the closed circuitry of signification. The substitution of cognitive voice for voice unmuted opens the book of knowledge which has been previously written and ready for perusal. Here is the glitter of found gold. Perhaps there are two books as Francis Bacon thought: divine Scripture and the book of created world. When voice speaks effectively, it mimics holy truth by reading with the mind's eye the record inscribed "in the littlest thing" by God's command. But beware of found things! While most found objects cost dearly, the price of speech is modesty itself. Ineffective voice, the serpent's tongue, voice with a weak and hollow ring: all are misreadings, intentional or otherwise. The only falseness is in the falsetto, the stutter, the hoarseness, the breathiness of the reading.

The reading voice (= speech) frames voice the way that a glove fits the hand; the nearly perfect aligning of contours. One almost forgets the simple act of reversal which yields a violent incongruity. Voice is the carrier wave for thought, breath is the mule of meaning. Phonocentrism is inverted, as I said, by the cough and the laugh. Add to the cast of characters the sneeze, the grunt (particularly from physical exertion), the wheeze, the clack (of the tongue, of dentures), the hiss, the cackle, the gasp (a vocal inspiration), the squeal, the squeak, the screech, and the peculiar unnamed sound of clearing the throat. When phonation is broken in the assault by this rogues' gallery, the body of the body issues audible vibration. The defense line collapses. The walled citadel keeping guerilla sounds *out* and cognitive ones *in* is overrun. The out is in, and the in is out. The distinction between carrier wave and signal, the master of meaning and the ass conveying the matter, gives way. The breath, unmodulated by broadcast articulation, bursts forth. One ceases cancelling the vibrating column of air in Aristotle's windpipe as extraneous noise. The unretained breath voices its degree of retention which is its freedom and freedom to the one who gives it voice. The hoarse, harsh breath *versus* the deeply rhythmic breath: the breath vociferously voices its matter which the body's life. The unchecked breath resonates to the measure of life taken against the silence of death. We have a sense of this familiar neglected sound in Stanley Kubrick's film *2001: A Space Odyssey* during an extended scene in which the audio is Keir Dullea's respiration in his spacesuit. Before the technology of larygneal contraction, one breathed for life. First and foremost, battering down the armor of spoken voice frees the breath. In the labile logic of reversal, the effect transposes the voice back to the breath. We the audience breathe easier when the speaker takes a deep, natural breath. The sound of the breath affirms its way of nonarticulating. In the movement of life between reversals, the acute listener can hear both breaths—retained and free, articulating and unphonemic—in any voicification. To that repeated involution the ear must turn.

The flip side to Aristotle's phonocentrism and its harnassing the breath is the uninstrumented windpipe. With utility, culturation, stabilization, and domestication come the opposition (nonuse, savagery, destabilization, the outcast) already poised for attack. To flip the idea, get the self-will out of the throat. If volition is in the largynx, it already is out of it. Negative phonocentrism already has a foothold as soon as one listens to the actual sound production process. Example: [Sound of throat-clearing] "Uh, I [grunt] [wheeze] want a [click] [inhalation] cup of coffee [sigh] [cough]." The economy of phonemic signs erases the disparity between actual voice production and its transcript. The interruption ceases to disturb history. Phonocentrism involves an economy of lack. Another opposition within phonocentrism—the spoken *(parole)* and the written *(langue)* language—explains away the missing element; I suggest below how to resist the ready answer. Revolution in the economy of desire, breath retention, largyneal mastery, deferred attention, and the technology of soul-talk overthrow the primary bastion of spoken voice. Control of the means of voice production ceases to be the object of desire. Cutting the voice free from the agent of the soul resident in the throat produces radically new and ephemeral alliances up and down the vocal register. The death of the "throat mind" ushers in a novel epoch. From the body of the body issues the voice of the voice.

The interruption of history is its inverting, dismembering, and reframing: the surface on which events are written undergoes a sudden topological transformation. Because of the elasticity of memory, interrupted history snaps back to its configuration of comfort. What becomes of the trace of discontinuity? No molecular imprint of it survives in the comfort zone. Vocal speech is a totality of relations so dense as to preclude (almost) anything but the fact of self-reference. What is said (indicated, declared, proclaimed, asserted, denied, equivocated over, debated, deduced, doubted, etc.) is kept in place by the gravitational pull of language. No voice escapes that must not be passed over in silence. Thus Plato in a slightly posterior context notices the impossibility "that written words can do anything more than remind one who knows that which the writing is concerned with." (*Phaedrus* 275d) What is the specific concern of a voice not for reading nor for the perpetuity of desire whose coin is signification? To what or to whom does such a voice address? To whom does it belong? That free voice provokes this skew line of question clues us to the breath's other aspect.

Startlingly the breath rattles in the gap of speech. Every respiration proves the discontinuity of spoken meaning. *That* deformation of spoken voice I now want to explore—with a creveat. I have no plan (congruent to speech's latent love of mutism) to discover a void of meaning (though one might). The initial phonemic revolution which begins the history of erasure installs cognition as the supreme and only spokesman for ideas. Mind is the mother tongue. The Greek infatuation with continence and the concept continues to instill fear of an unreason present just beyond the proposition's closure. A breath of freedom unmasks the idea that ideas—simple or abstract—wear a uniform which is thought, mental activity, and cognition. Our love of ideas goes just so far, to the point that we feel uncomfortable. In the scheme of things, ideas—eternal objects—wear the dress of many pursuits, bodily kinetics, musical harmony (and disharmony), graphic art, and dramatic interaction, to name a few. Ideas exist peculiar to gustation, olefaction, and tactility though many are lost. Being convinced that a costume change does not change character is part of Rousseau's conviction about interchangeable organs of communication:

> The art of communicating our ideas depends less upon the organs we use in such communication than it does upon a power proper to man, according to which he uses his organs in this way, and which, if he lacked these, would lead him to use others to the same end. (*Essay*, p. 10)

The replaceable, dispensable, disposal *thing* belongs to the same technology as a phonemics isomorphic in meaning to soul-talk. If all ideas have a mental proxy, a representative within the central citadel, nonverbal ideas are all expendable. Improperly dressed, they have long ago been written out of the book of knowledge. Why talk about them now? Thus the tone of the technological imperative: the tautened glottis of refusal. But drop the economy of desire which designates the dress code for ideas, and the shoeless horde comes back to hound the mind into realization or madness. Among this rabble is the voice, the means of producing human sound. Of the noncognitive mediums of ideas, the voice of voice is no more nor less articulate than others (kinesis or music), which is to say, not articulate at all until the technology of sound production is freed of its retentive, exploitive, domineering aspect. But before I consider reframed voice, the voice of vocal transmission of ideas, the voice of voice, much effort must be spent on the matter of retention. To this I now turn.

CHAPTER 4

THE VERGE OF MADNESS

To reframe the thought patterns centering on human voice is to recenter the ellipses which invisibly define the historical account of voice. The subtractions add immeasurable clarity to the being of voice. Let me show some of what has been stolen from the phenomenon. The ascension of speech—phonemic voice—as pretender to the throne of voicification is clearly marked in Hobbes. He says:

> But the most noble and profitable invention of all other, was that of *speech*, consisting of *names* or *appellations*, and their connection; whereby men register their thoughts, recall them when they are past, and also declare them one to another for mutual utility and conversation; without which there had been amongst men neither commonwealth, nor society, nor contract, nor peace, no more than amongst lions, bears, and wolves. (*Leviathan* IV)[1]

The *act* of investing phonemics with the full power of voice is, on Hobbes' view, the arche-act of the polis. Anarchy, the state of irresolvable conflict of one person against the other, is thereby defeated. Speech displaces self-gratification with the need for "conversation," literally meant, "for persons keeping company with one another." Capitalizing on mutual interests, the social contract is framed tacitly, then explicitly. Persons cease to prey upon one another like wild brutes only when their speaking reminds them ceaselessly of the adverse consequences of inhibiting conversation. The leviathan itself is a seed word in a fluid and fluent mother tongue. Its representations, concerns, infrastructure, and form of life take their nourishment from that amniotic, the phoneme. Take speech away and personal relations devolve back to the elemental sounds of narcissism. What is the name of the human sound which, for Hobbes, speech transcends, whose exclusion is the condition *sine qua non* for political survival? Not the sound of the predator—lion, bear, or wolf—for men are not driven by the same organic condition of the carnivore, but by self-aggrandisement and self-love. Fear of bodily attack is not the terminus of fear since that fear neither paralyzes nor strikes one dumb; it alerts and activates the inborn defenses. The sound that the phonemic state rids people of is madness. A single fear closes the fatal breech in conversation and perpetuates the state—fear of insanity. Hobbes' state rids the earth of crazed phonation. It fortifies human voice against the voice of unreason.

Momentary loss of speech threatens the onslaught of madness. To babble is, as Hobbes warns, to repeat the loss of what was "lost at the Tower of Babel, when, by the hand of God, every man was stricken, for his rebellion, with an oblivion of his former language."[2] Civil rebellion is always rebellion against phonemic authority. It is rebellion against the need to engage in the conversation which, moment to moment, constructs the civil state from the matter of conflict and chaos. What is Hobbes' state of war? Primordially *not* each man appropriating according to selfish desire and therefore against the other, since no state can eliminate the ego's drive. Instead, the state-implemented peace annuls an absence which is the absence of the means of appropriation themselves. In "war," no person is capable of identifying and trying to secure the object of his or her desire. Hence conflict (which would be plentiful) is vain, aimless, and without furtherance of anyone over anyone else. In the state of war, conflict throws one back on the war against oneself, of the greater against the lesser, of the stupid against the self-recognized. Victory in this conflict aims at self-realization. That which is defeated is the ego and the ego's tongue. Along the way, struggle needs to undo fixity, rigid attitude, retention, and self-deceit.

Phonemic control, the speaking of words, subdues a reality at odds with fixed designation. Undesignated reality, the world unperceivable in categories—the coin of reason—poses a dire threat to the convocation of citizens. Because reality is at war with any partition into signs, it threatens to undo not the fact but the possibility of commerce. A single person remains at war as long as no measure of exchange exists. Take two persons in communication, and for Hobbes, the possibility of measure is born. Common language, conversation, supposes common measure, shared sensation, interpretation, and signification. Annul them and primordial war recurs. Human warfare, the brutishness of man living according to nature, derives from lack of name and appellation. The warlord's voice merely vociferates each person's immediate response to all-encompassing reality. Immediacy makes for irremedial difference, hence, derangement of the *vox populi*. Speech ushers in the Great Peace. Speech pacifies by providing means of judging immediacies and proportioning the economy of desire. Speech staves off the maddening flux of reality which sets no limits to the sensory appropriation preceding commerce. It thereby restores humanity to its "sanity." In Hobbes's equation, conversation = political economy, the hidden integer is sanity. Subtract it from other side and we have war.

The war cry is crazed by virtue of its immunity to phonemic regulation. One could, with Homer (or the cartoonist), say, "Aeeiii!" But what happens to the blood curdling, the breath stuck in the gullet, or the taste of hot metal on the tongue? Heavy pretense draws the cry of battle into spoken voice. This shows by relief the power of belief when we almost hear the sound. The authority of the phonemic lies in the control of a brutish organism and its responsive voicing of events. The leviathan is spawned in this single act of subjugation. Like all acts of love, its consummation is blind. In its moment lies the blindspot in Hobbes' thought. Let us try to see it. The potent invisibility of the germ emerges in his later denial of the state's insemination. If order breeds concord, then discord must breed derangement. The blindness of love is to rectify (erase) all history that disclaims its pure passion. For Hobbes, the prehistory of the civil state, "nature," cannot contain madness because "Nature itself cannot err; and as men abound in copiousness of language, so they become more wise, or more mad, than ordinary." (*Leviathan* V)[3] The history before the history that Hobbes rewrites contains no error because it contains no truth. In order to save the State, that creature of love, Hobbes reshapes the matter of truth. Where truth becomes a trophy of phonemic conquest, "the right ordering of names in our affirmations," "natural history"

remains neutral with respect to veracity and falsehood. (*Leviathan* IV)[4]
Without knowing it, Hobbes's precivil history defends against a
fragility at the heart of conversation. It protects the vulnerability of
the beast's body.

What does it take to shatter the compact? Each of us knows the
voice of extremity, disconsolation, anguish, or imbecility. "Pillicock
sat on Pillicock-hill. Alow; alow, loo, loo!" mad Edgar utters to Lear.
The night is one of madness, a violent storm, bedlam's hovel, a senile
king, a fool for a companion, and a prince disguised as an inmate of
Bedlam. Edgar takes us back to a pre-Hobbesian condition of war.
Conversation fragments along one of its several dimensions. Edgar
offers a Trojan horse to the civil state. Opened, its contents—
ungrammatical, dis-semantic radicals, returning sound production to
the madness of primordial war—promise to slew the sleeping citizens
of speech. "Alow, alow, loo, loo!" finds the exact heart of Hobbes'
speechification and stabs at it without mercy. A new fact concerning
Hobbes is revealed to us. The primary passion prostrating people at
the altar of peace and phonemic authority is fear of death. (*Leviathan*
XIII)[5] Hobbes might well have added its equally dark companion, fear
of insanity.

Madness, conversation (civil and interior), the phoneme, and the
polis exert gravitational pulls on human sound production. Speech is
an act perpetually reinvesting political power in itself—though
inarticulately since it is forever incapable of articulating its organic,
prepolitical origin. It must continuously replace the maddening war of
opposites with itself and itself be replaced, or else speech will be struck
dumb by the point of nonreplacement and the whole system fall
silently to the ground. That point is known only to intimacy whose
silence is terrifying, joyful, or both. Now add to this fragile position
the fact that the life-form of the phoneme is corruptible. Its vibratory
body, the profile of matter locally resonating at a specific frequency, is
vulnerable to distortion. The motives appear for the sizeable arma-
ments that speaking keeps against the unspoken voice. The cough, the
laugh, the unthrottled breath, the battle cry each may threaten the
contrived contour of the phoneme. Sanity lives or dies with the fragile
control exerted cognitively over the organs of speech. The brutishly
misshapen phoneme—the grotesquery of sound—is ever ready to
vanquish the noble spirit of the spoken word in the heat of passion,
the nightmare, physical illness and torture, and acute sufferings. The
pax vocalis ends at any instant with the organism's audible upsurge. A
sigh will do. By the same token, we can reread Hobbes's notion of

animality with new understanding. "Lions, bears, and wolves" are warring beasts not because they are animals but because they lack the phoneme. Given the power of speech, as in the Christmas fable, they become peaceful, law-abiding, God-fearing creatures of reason. The dilemma for the phonocentric statesman is to silence the animal in man, the uncouth noises of bear and lion which roll unexpectedly from the tip of the tongue. To this end exists the state of glottal tension and respiratory re-tention. They are the weapons on active alert against vocalic subversion.

I began with a lacuna in Hobbes' thought concerning the speaking of speech. The political dimension fails to appear on either side of the formula, "speech = pacification by names." In "this war of every man against every man" in which *"nothing can be unjust,"* phonological truce must be reinstituted by the continual repetition of habit. Conversation supplies the missing criteria of justice. When persons speak in a common tongue, barter, distribution, and decision become possible. The total lack of a *gesture* of fairness, for Hobbes, has less to do with absent virtues of justice than with the absence of articulation. For even the lions know how to divvy up the kill. And the wolves stick to a strict order of just deserts over the prey. In the state of war, the unjustness is premoral, not amoral. The lack can never be filled by a moral sense which is prehistory. Salvation depends solely on the mentalization of "names and appellations," the registry of thought. Mind alone stops the Heraclitean demolition of one sound by its opposite and contemplates the vision of perpetual peace. To establish the polis, mind-work must proceed by abstraction. Each sound conjures its opposite. Each sound on the scale of harmony contains all other sounds. High contains low, soft contains brash, cowardly contains courageous. To ensure political survival and institute the history of the contract, sound can no longer sound the clash of voice against voice. Sound must be made soundless.

The authority of silence and its defense against madness and war impose exile on voice. Saussure completes the thought:

> It is impossible for sound alone, a material element, to belong to language. It is only a secondary thing, substance to be put to use. All our conventional values have the characteristic of not being confused with the tangible element which supports them. (Saussure II.IV.3)[6]

Turning the volume down to zero on speech, Saussure distils a mental essence from the physical act of sound production. Thereafter, the intellectual theory of signs disposes of the particular acoustic contour in favor of the signifying reflex. "The idea of phonic substance that a sign contains is of less importance than the other signs that surround it."[7] Only now, the political content of the muting and mutilation of vocalic speech is thoroughly camoflaged. The polis lies hidden in the environment of cooperating (and coopting) signs. The leviathan acquires symbolic value. The imposition of linguistic capability over the prehistorical function of the organs of speech (palatal, glottal, and pneumatic)—their "phonic substance"—is erased before the subject. Derangement is removed from the political body in the way that the living animal is cut from butcher's meat. Saussure presumes that uncivil voice is never just (reason's highest virtue) because it is just sound. History begins with spoken justice because the barter of wolves and lions is pure force, instinct, or whimsy. It provides us with no record. The muscular and nervous control of voice, therefore, is not a proper object of study: "The question of the vocal apparatus obviously takes a secondary place in the problem of language." (Saussare, Introduction III.1)[8] It is unstately. His is companion to Hume's approach. Perception pares sensation from organic intelligence and relegates its study "more to anatomists and natural philosophers than to moral."[9]

From the displaced political act arises the Saussurean distinction of *parole* and *langue*. *Langue*, "a self-contained whole and a principle of classification," is nonetheless "concrete, no less so than *parole*." (Saussure, Introduction III.2)[10] Concreteness for *langue* as well as *parole* is not a matter of presentational immediacy, direct contact with raw fact. It is the act of political embodiment, of placing signs at the disposal of the organ which the state provides. The ongoing signifying conversation of one person with the other concretely constitutes the moment-to-moment continuation of political reality, which is to say, vocalic reality, reality period. Lumping the concrete event with the political act of signifying inverts the prehistorical picture. Not only is *langue*, the symbolic form actualizing speech, *as concrete* as *parole*; it is the source of all that is tangible, brute, immediate, undeniable, irrefutable. By contrast, *parole* wanes in reality-content. It may be essentially real (by virtue of partaking in the symbolizing form) but contains messy, material (i.e., apolitical) substance. Saussure:

> Linguistic signs are tangible; it is possible to reduce them to conventional written symbols, whereas it would be impossible to provide detailed photographs of acts of speaking [*actes de parole*]; the pronuncia-

tion of even the smallest word represents an infinite number of muscular movements that could be identified and put into graphic form only with great difficulty. (Saussure, Introduction III.3)[11]

When we replace the political element elided in Saussure, what does speech, *parole*, become? It is the perogative of the citizen to execute what *langue* legislates. "Execution is always individual, and the individual is always its master: I shall call the executive side *speaking* [*parole*]." (Ibid.) Compare Hobbes: "The sovereign is the soul of the commonwealth; which once departed from the body, the members do no more receive their motion from it." (*Leviathan* XXI)[12] Speaking (*parole*) is political rule by nomenclature *(langue)*. Since no form of ruling exists other than by appellation and name, to speak is to assume the part of sovereign. The speaker seizes the same political power over his or her organism as the monarch, oligarch, or tyrant does over the body politic. The spoken word repeats the magical power which ceaselessly recreates the republic from natural chaos. Bye the bye, the spoken word institutes the rule of *lex naturalis* ("a precept or general rule, found out by reason") which remains curiously inert in the state of war. As long as one speaks, aloud or *sotto voce*, one retains political and moral (i.e., cognitive) power over the amoral, chthonic forces of the body. For, as all mental things, the "laws of nature are immutable and eternal; for injustice, ingratitude, arrogance, pride, iniquity, acception of persons, and the rest, can never be made lawful." (*Leviathan* XV)[13] When speech departs from the body, death comes to the sovereign. War returns. What limits *parole* in keeping the unbridled force of the soma at bay? No limit of abuse or violence exists. In investing absolute power, Hobbes calls on the absolute:

> Nothing the sovereign representative can do to a subject on what pretense soever, can properly be called injustice, or injury; because every subject is author of every act the sovereign doth; so that he never wanteth right to anything, other than he himself is the subject of God, and bound thereby to observe the laws of nature. (*Leviathan* XXI)[14]

Speaking may even require the death of the vocal subject, not only in the obvious case of treason. It does just that in every case that throttles the war cry. And the "laws of nature" themselves? In giving the "first and fundamental law of nature; which is, *to seek peace and follow it*," Hobbes omits telling us the precondition of seeking anything whatsoever. (*Leviathan* XIV)[15] To identify (and thereby to be able to seek) requires us to name. The laws of nature are housed in human nomenclature, in *langue*. Being God's subject and giving speech the power of life and death over voice means being subject to the claims of language. *Langue*, God, natural law, and reason occupy the four corners of one and the same quadrilateral, comprising the walls of the polis. Take one away and the barbarians return.

Security of the citadel has one important breech. The subject— the vocalness of voice—is left out. For safety's sake the quirk of control avoids being involved in the contingent. Thus only accidently does speech involve human voice. For Saussure (as for Aristotle) its potential for existence (as *langue*, the cortical storehouse of sound-images) is greater than its actuality, the raw effulgence of sound. Its higher value lies in the catalogue. Language, the legislative gazette, gives class to the world. Adam, the First Man's greatness consists in applying the list of names to things. Hobbes: "The first author of speech was God himself, that instructed Adam how to name such creatures as He presented to his sight." (*Leviathan* IV)[16] Both state and language come into being by the selfsame act of reference. *Parole*, the lesser, deficient by virtue of "phonic substance," never provides the barricade to keep the wolves outside the gate. Part of its inferiority stems from its moral nature. Being conditioned by muscle and blood, it lives in its vulnerability to life. Speech proper also remains inferior due to a conflict which Hobbes keeps well hidden. Spoken voice strives to execute the absolute peace-making power (its inheritance) while, being of the person, it is born in the state of war. Naturally, speech desires to speak the needs that war creates. But war surpasses the limits of reason and can never be spoken without encountering the forbidden—without speaking madness. Thus what spoken voice wants to say is already at a distance from what can be said. *Parole* disturbs the calm phonetics classroom like the maddening lust of an outlaw on a warm spring day.

The deficiency (phonation as the effect of the organism) haunts the Saussarian-Hobbesian defense of voice against madness. Spoken voice is real vibratory response. It lacks the immune system of an abstract object *(langue)* to attack, invasion, insurrection, and the subsequent negotiated truce or capitulation. Error in production, the slip of the tongue, a spoonerism, an unwanted pun, all become the neurotic preclude to true psychosis. Because the mouth is lacking in sanitation, spoken voice is suspect in sanity. Look by contrast at a systematic inventory of "sound-images," fixed for all time. It is free from a person's foolishness or derangement. It cannot become unhinged in violent animal frenzy, Edgar's "Flibbertigibbet." Vulnerable, speech may well betray the cognitive self-will. The betrayal, moreover, is one by the lower of the higher, not the reverse. The madness which is object of fear is not divine ecstasy nor sacrifice to a more perfect mind. Divine madness or enlightened idiocy is precluded by the covenant. For by politicizing the relation of name to referent and placing it at the center of human voice, one creates the dread alliance between animality (the lower) and insanity. The Axis powers line up against the Allies of reason and civil society.

We catch herein the secret contradiction of the leviathan. Abolition of civil society reveals man as an animal lower than the lion, bear, or wolf because man falls to that condition. he does not come by nature to it. For Hobbes, the original situation of humanity, the war of contradictories, is inferior because it is crazed. To be thrown back on the struggle to acquire an individual existence is to be in the asylum. To respond vocally to the exigence of self-recognition surpasses the limits of sanity. War literally is madness. The insane's animal voice—shrieking, screaming, growling, or grunting unphonemic syllables—is the crazed ejaculation of vocification. The world echoes with such sound before the advent of justice. Foucault takes note of the grim fact:

> The animality that rages in madness dispossesses man of what is specifically human in him; not in order to deliver him over to other powers, but simply to establish him at the zero degree of his own nature.[17]

The lupine creature which Hobbes seeks to keep beyond the walls shows itself to inhabit an interior and natural terrain. The wolf resounds in the unfettered vibrations of the voice box during strange, uncivil interludes. These moments correspond to a vocalic search for consciousness of humanity.

Speech has greatness, being "the most noble and profitable invention of all other." The greatness is, for Hobbes, reason itself, "that is adding and subtracting, of the consequences of general names agreed upon for the marking and signifying of our thoughts." (*Leviathan* V)[18] As great is speech in its power of commanding the organs, it is greater in denial. Speech lives denying that which it, in signifying, replaces. It manages a system of signifiers which, one by one, can replace each other. But of the fundamental signified, which is nonreplaceable, it must refuse knowledge. Speech, as I have said, must dwell in the pacified zone. Where no markers exist, at that point consumed by the war which would destroy at a single blow the whole system of signs, it cannot touch. The point is at once spoken and denied by all speaking. Spoken voice in this way repeats the contradictory state of war. The flip side of denial is desire. What speech, on the Hobbes-Saussure view, desires is to embrace its origin in war. But that point, the matrix of opposition, is constantly annihilating the context of itself. Speech wishes to touch and be touched by what it eludes at every moment, the mothering of meaning. The desire to speak unreason and illogic is greatest in the throes of passion, inspiration, and awe, when eros, art, and religion conspire to produce the incoherent sounds of our full humanity. But here, we are speechless, though not mute. Speech may attend the initial breakthrough or the final leavetaking of the point, if lovers' words, the poets', or the devotees' are testimony. It is *as if* we had spoken the point. The point itself, however, escapes articulation like an event which never properly takes place. Hence, on the Hobbes-Saussure view, speech remains perpetually unconsummated, yet consummated in its lack.

To speak is, I said, to call the unspoken—anarchy and madness—to desire. Unspeakable passion or wonder does not thereby exemplify the desire which Hobbes erases from the history of voice. They are soft, "womanly," nonaggressive states while war confronts the name with "manly" violence. To contact anarchical desire, we need to return to the original breech in the state of nature created by the justice of the word-sound. At the origin, the need for conversation replaces the need to be victorious in the war of opposition. Denotation replaces fatuity, what Hobbes calls "metaphors, and senseless and ambiguous words [which] are like *ignes fatui*."[19] He fails to indicate that fatuity falls steeply away into dementia and that metaphor plunges suddenly into imbecilic frenzy. His broad-stroke sketches of precivil, prehistoric humanity are notoriously sentimental, his epigram of life being "solitary, poor, nasty, brutish, and short" notwithstanding. The intent to stress the evil consequences of human self-will amounts to a nostalgia of the ego. It provides disinformation about the natural economy of desire as soon as we remember the equation, war = madness. Application of that formula reframes the original replacements and allows us to recognize that going mad is, for Hobbes, the revolutionary act par excellence. Madness returns the person to the primordial state of humanity before the polis.

In each spoken act, we butt against the unspeakable desire

forbidden by conversation, the arche-political act of keeping company with the other. The dark desire is for revolution, to stop making sense in the use of voice, and to give voice to the lion, bear, or wolf lurking just beyond the walls of cognitive construction. Persons' speaking draws impulse from the wish to cease all signifying, each token of which reforges, in Hobbes's luminous image,

> artificial chains, called *civil laws*, which they themselves, by mutual covenants, have fastened, at one end to the lips of that man or assembly to whom they have given the sovereign power, and at the other end to their own ears. (*Leviathan* XXI)[20]

The formidable urge toward phonemic production illuminates the central place fear holds in Hobbes's scheme. Fear which in war serves to disperse persons, one from the other and from the self, is not transformed in pacification by speech. Instead, it remains fear, but now bearing its proud name, gathers humanity together in the commonwealth in the same manner in which a general term gathers particulars from the dispersed chaos. Fear is lability, changefulness itself, and change, that which in war is most feared. Prepolitical fear which kept men apart is now pooled in its fluid form and directed against a single man, the sovereign. Before political society, people fear loss of power, afterwards, loss of the ruler who safeguards the continued power of conversation. In this vein, Hobbes expresses his loathing of regicide or even tyrannicide (*Leviathan* XXIX)[21]—revolution drawn to its anarchical conclusion—which amounts to the death of speech, "what manner of life there would be, where there were no common power to fear." (*Leviathan* XIII)[22] In assassinating him who embodies language and from whom speech disseminates, the polis degenerates into mad acts and utterances. By inversion, fear of madness serves a most important political purpose. Fear is the instrument which persecutes the rebel, the one who would relax phonemic control and allow voice to express real and basic needs of the vocalizing being. The leviathan pacifies by means of fear and fears anyone who makes peace with fear.

Prehistorical fear disperses, political fear unifies. Desire in the polis keeps people together in an economy of conversational competition. What about prehistorical, primordial desire? The one who transforms his or her "natural" reaction to fear, regardless of the object and who is able to live neither affirming nor denying it glimpses that desire. Fear which is fear of lability surrounds the native changeability of what a person desires. One fears that a known quantity will become unknown, that attainment will not gratify, that nonattainment will cause suffering. Because the person, the experience, and the object of desire never remain fixed, desire belongs to the condition which Hobbes calls war. The equilibrium of the triadic relation constituting desire is an unstable one. The "natural" (= political) reaction to the unstability, in Hobbes's scheme, is rigidification by fear. A person who lives in lability is free from fear. The rest turn toward the strategy of recasting change in the mold of fear and grow fearful of desire, or what amounts to the same thing, grow desirous of fear. We have seen the great birth such desire begets: phonemic voice, the polis, cognition, even God. But to embrace the shapeshifting balance and neutralize the "nature" of fear is to encounter desire per se. Such desire, we may now notice, is not the political hybrid, but one bred of prepolitical humanity. Not transmogrified by the need for conversation, it is desire born *of* war but not *for* war.

A cold look at fear allows one to correct the reversed polarities. Before and after becoming politicized and institutionalized, the economy of desire is fear. The difference lies in concentrating the means of production in the speech-making sovereign. For Hobbes, if fear did not exist, neither would speaking. Thus, fear is not an invention of speech, "that most noble and profitable invention," but its double, the other face that phonemic authority can never observe. The fear that one could speak no more (death) or that one could speak no more sense (madness) is not a device of conversation, to keep the company up. Both are its shadows, its phantasms, which appear in dreams and nightmares and which disappear in the release from phonemic sovereignty. Under the authority of speaking, however, no space exists between their referential reality and their institutionalized value. Both are the keel and the rudder under which the ship of state sails. This explains why to let go the voice encounters the enormity of fear before all else. The war waged by desire no longer mutated by fear is not waged for mere self-aggrandizement, as Hobbes's economy has it. It is the war of oneself pitted against oneself for the purpose of recovering the self. Hobbes's warriors who "live without other security than what their own strength and there own invention shall furnish them withal," are already police officers of the polis. (*Leviathan* XIII)[23] Their war is not the primordial human condition but one consequent to a treaty of surrender. Speechmakers, they have already turned from the struggle of self-actualization. Perhaps, they have turned from the initial barricade, the political betrayal of our organism, especially of the organs of speech.

"My wits begin to turn," Lear declares, "Come on my boy." In the onslaught of his madness lies the demise of the sovereign state and the reign of kingly speech. Lear's immediate concern ("How dost, my boy? Art cold? I am cold myself.") redirects him to the organic base of his hitherto regal existence. He is on the way to confronting his fear of insanity and the horde of passions accompanying it, of letting go the reins of phonemic control, and of desiring his real desire. We may recognize precisely what must be lived through and suffered before voice again gains voice. What apocalypse waits on the far side of fear—dementia, death, solitude, or muteness—must be known and recognized as the natural progeny of the fundamental signifier, the nonreplaceable point on which all civil life rests. The origin of speech, the breath check and retention of glottal control, reinstituted moment after moment, must be confronted and understood. Only then does the question arise, *whose* voice is it? The force of that question quietens apprehension of madness, mortality, isolation, or silence. It overthrows the economy of desire which argues that fear alone serves to circumvent human solitude and beget the leviathan. Lear gives a dramatic response to the question. Facing his weakness, he rejects the voice of sovereignity (magisterial command of "phonic substance") in favor of his own voice. With the revolution in his voicing, the polis collapses.

Does the recovery of voice, arising with the recovery of the self which voices, mean the end of the life of the polis? Is there a basis to people's life together under law—a new republic—which can be discovered on fear's far side? These questions rise from the ashes of political society. Much sifting is needed before I discover the remains of life in them.

CHAPTER 5

THE METAPHOR OF VOICE

The history of voice makes a peculiar omission. The beastly cough, an event of voice, is not included. Similarly, with other beasts (the sneeze, the burp, the gargle). How do manifest human sounds become muted by the philosopher? When we listen more closely, we find political intent behind the act of erasure. Each and every deletion repeats the history. The deleted matter must predate and coexist with the act of deletion. The lie is that all history lies because each spoken (or written) history serves a polis. The truth recognizes that political history (all history) cannot hide its revisionist intent for long. The fact of concealment is a fact whose erasure proves its truth. I review this fact because Hobbes's version of political history has the virtue of clarity. I have spent time with his rendition of the proto-act of the polis: the dynasty of speech installed over the organs of voice. By the law of repetition, each act of speaking—interior or public—reconstitutes the original political covenant. Interruption of speech making threatens to uncover the erasure. Thus any interruption provokes repression and retention—the agents of phonemic authority which maintain the economy of fear. The revolutionary, most feared in the sovereign kingdom of speech, wears the identity of the madman. He alone breaks the cognitive hold on the breath and glottis, liberates inarticulate and brutish sounds from his body, and negates the civil state at its origin. His attack on the signifier-signified relation is the most significant antipolitical act. Its effect is to retrieve the world from the political history. He reawakens the vital, somatic heart of voice, hitherto subdued by the taut structure of the phoneme.

Without the revolt, the civil economy of desire invariably leads to solitude. On this score, Hobbes is clearer than Husserl who naively propounds interior soliloquy as the model for speaking, thereby failing to penetrate to the political basis of solitariness. Solitude is a negative which is a minus. No mutation of its logic will yield community. The leviathan is a monstrous hybrid for this reason. In appearance it seems a unity, but in fact the only unification—of fear—is conglomeration. A new basis for the body politic, one which would grant freedom to the voice of voice, must arise from another direction. To uncover it, we need further to scrutinize how political retentiveness is called into being. I want to deepen the wedge opening the equation, voice = speech, with an ear to the sounds which may thereafter erupt.

The amniotic which gives birth both to the polis and the word-sounds looks like the point of origin. Hobbes does not tell us that conception preceeds birth. What is our vocal life before beginning conversation? We return to the intense ambiguity of experience, of reality stinging our sensitive membranes with the demand for response. At that time, to engage conversation is already a loss in responsiveness, in expressibility, in vocalic quality. We are not mute, for the exclamatory power of our existence is at a zenith. In the dark woods, not knowing what entity interrogates us, we open our mouths to speak only for distraction's sake. Just as standing is, anatomically speaking, a perpetual flight from falling, so is phonemic articulation, vocally speaking, a perpetual flight from the truth. What happens at the originary point? When we look to Hobbes for an account, we find ourselves already past it. With his characteristic fixity of mind, he tries to make up for the lack with a rigidifying distinction. This moment is for him of great import. It is his contact with the law of concealment. Instead of a primordial responsiveness to the reality of the perception, Hobbes separates the voluntary from the automatic. Rather than focus on fusing of the germ cells of human voice and society, he acts prophylactically to prevent insemination. This explains the mon-strosity of the leviathan. It arises from barren seed by partheno-genesis.

Let us inspect his account. "There be in animals," he begins.

> two sorts of *motions* peculiar to them: one called *vital*, begun in generation and continued without interruption through their whole life; such as are the course of the blood, the pulse, the breathing, the concoction, nutrition, excretion, etc., to which motions there needs no help of imagination: the other is *animal motion*, otherwise called *voluntary motion*; as to go, to speak, to move any of our limbs, in such manner as is first fancied in our minds. (*Leviathan* VI)[1]

Animals, ensouled creatures whose life "is but a motion of limbs," contain two complementary processes. The vital, self-sustaining, self-regulating, continuous, warm feminine functionings of the organism constitute one type of movement. They require no cognitive support for effective operation, and so, in a strained metaphor, are likened to automata, "engines that move themselves by springs and wheels as doth a watch." (*Leviathan*, Introduction)[2] The second kind of process, interventionary, sporadic, self-willed, chilling masculine operation of cognition, is found in animals, the human animal, and artificial beings like the leviathan. The apparent coupling of one with the other—voluntary motion—in the case of the vocal apparatus, yields the now-famous articulated sound. The voluntary in general lives in the consummatory activity of the two. The warm vital processes accept the chilling entry of cognition. Speech, the state of conversation, the political state, and all its arts and sciences are the heralded children of this most fruitful union.

From the start, Hobbes is hobbled by an equivocation respecting "animal motion" which raises doubts about the marital bed. He confesses uncertainty about the intelligent cooperation of the vital. He views the breath and the pulse as unreceptive mechanical operations, unwilling to let pass the active mind. This attitude makes it necessary to rely upon the hidden equation, cognition = God's will. Thus the fiat, "Let us make speech," serves the same purpose as God in human creation. *(Ibid.)* Such an entry is not welcome but forced from on high. The forced entry has an untoward result. Speech is no child of a human relation, the organic with the mental, but a child of supernal command. Like all messengers of divine imperative, speech is on a messianic mission: to transform reality in the light of an ideal. It is not the invention that Hobbes acclaims but inventor. Speech makes stories up which we come to accept as true.

One such tale is of its own conception. Even if we believe that the cognitive joins with the vital, serious questions surround the circumstances of union. If God's act enters man as speech, our spark is that of contradiction. The act is source of the effacement and erasure which speech suffers in betraying the solicitations of the real. To speak is, as already said, to effect the decline of voice. The framing of articulation embodies, for Hobbes, the initial contradiction. It is a cause of decadence and retention yet at the same time of "the most noble and profitable invention." The nobility and degradation both derive in voluntary union from the help afforded phonemic authority by the imagination. If that help were of love ("of one singularly, with desire to be singularly beloved"), we would expect the imagination to bestow recognition on the organic functionings. (*Leviathan* VI)[3] Instead, the vital energies are further veiled from view. Their integral role in knowledge is confused. The obscuration indicates shame ("grief for the discovery of some defect of ability").[4] Shame could not have the vital processes as its object since they are adequate to their operations of self-maintenance and -regulation. The shame which brings together a warm vitality and a cold mind must derive from the perception which the imagination has secretly of itself. Speech and all of voluntary motion is marked and marred by the abhorrent vision that the imagination withholds of its own identity.

Why does the imagination's help corrupt? The imagination, Hobbes tells us, is a power of retention. "For after the object is removed, or the eye shut, we still retain an image of the things seen, though more obscure than when we see it." (*Leviathan* II)[5] To retain is to make dim. It is to lose the power of discriminating origins, which is why for Hobbes it operates equally in dreaming and in waking. It is to hold on to what is left over, a remainder. Sensory experience, by contrast, knows the external body as its own prolongation, not as an extra. In the short life of sensation, one knows the origin of the object to be outside of itself. Sensation leaves no remainder since contact with the object entirely consumes it. It also is a pressure against an internal resistance (or "counterpressure"), an opposing current within vital motion. Hobbes proposes what Condillac later elaborates, that touch is the model of all sensation. In its logic of duality, sensory experience cannot leave off the point of contact between the external, originating force and vital motion without annulling itself. A relation with warm, self-sustaining organic processes never dims nor grows stale unless violated by a bearer of those qualities.

Enter the retentive imagination. In purporting to help vital motion to rise to the voluntary, it receives no vivifying influence of the body. The point is obscure to Hobbes. The only life brought to the marriage comes from the organic partner. The retentiveness of imagination is purely mechanical, strictly analogous to "as we see in the water, though the wind cease, the waves give not over rolling for a long time after." (*Leviathan* II)[6] The imagination holds on to an image of the world pressing sensorily in against our vital membranes, but the image is not fresh, cannot be fresh, intrinsically lacks the force of fresh contact. The desire of imagination is to keep something past present. Its accomplishment is to keep something decayed present. "Imagination therefore is nothing but *decaying sense*; and is found in men, and many other living creatures, as well sleeping as waking."[7] What imagination brings to its conjunction with vitality is feebleness, degeneracy, and ruin.

The dimness of perception surrounding the imagination is shame itself, "the discovery of some defect of ability." (*Leviathan* VI)[8] The marriage whose name is voluntary motion is one, not of love nor convenience, but of shame. To try to retain what is perishable is vain ("a well grounded confidence begetteth attempt, whereas the supposing of power does not, and is therefore rightly called *vain*").[9] Obscuration is built into the logic of retention, as Hobbes says, "the imagination of the past is obscured and made weak, as the voice of a man is in the noise of the day." (*Leviathan* II)[10] What is shameful is the pretence of control, the hubris that replaces the freshness of vital contact with the decayed trace left of its body. What the imagination discovers and must keep hidden from itself is that its retentive ability is in fact null. The sole thing that the imagination manages to retain is concealment of discovery. The shame of the imagination is and must remain secret like a venereal disease brought to stain the purity of a virgin's bed.

What is known of shame? Shame is not effaced by inattention. It rather becomes a displaced center of action invisibly infecting each and every movement with the signature of a disease. Hobbes's recognition of the pathology of imagination is, interestingly, restricted to instances ostensibly lacking volition, namely to dreams which "are caused by the distemper of some of the inward parts of the body."[11] The defect impels the analysis in this direction. The discovery which the mind knows and does not admit to knowing—its shame—relocates the pathology in an innocent process, dreaming. What could be less involved with self-will than the dream? Yet what can speak more clearly of the ego? In fact the pathological condition with which the imagination infects the voluntary is general and pervasive. Once the compliant, receptive vital functionings succumb to the alliance, the volition of shame is formed. Hobbes's condition of solitary humanity is but another name for human shame.

The wedding of the cognitive imagination and the vital energy of the body's interior processes no doubt bears fruit. Humanly speaking, the consummatory act unleashes volition upon the world. From the beginning, the absolute control of the self-will is triumphant. The chilling, dominant, intermittent force of imagination effaces the warm, receptive, sensitive power of the organism. The voice (or any bodily movement when not cognitively minded) is not human, is not voluntary, is not voice:

> And because going, speaking, and the like voluntary motions depend always upon a precedent thought of *whither, which way,* and *what;* it is evident that the imagination is the first internal beginning of all voluntary motion. (*Leviathan* VI)[12]

Because volition is conceived in shame and born heir to shame, the logic of desire is conspiracy and machination. The secret grief, the discovery of defect which must remain hidden, the concealed pain of any action: these passions propel the agent to plot out carefully beforehand the course and consequences of an endeavor. The reason that deliberates is the most important accomplice to shame; "the whole sum of desires, aversions, hopes, and fears, continued till the thing be either done or thought impossible, is that we call *delibera-tion.*"[13] We enter the circle of frenzy. Desire not monitored, inspected, surveyed, or prearranged is perilous. Are not the madman's desires those which have become unhinged from the deliberating censor? They are those which reveal the imagination's shame. Therefore, they provoke a revolt against the iron rule of reason. The voice which voices these made desires, the sound production of the insane, Edgar's "Aloo, aloo!": this too voices treason against the voluntary, speech, and political society. Free, spontaneous, joyful expression of the voice is not so much excluded from the voluntary as held to be an impolitic perversion, a gross anomaly, a grotesquery, an abortion. In this general way, shame protects itself from self-discovery by the device of obscuration. Hobbes, however, obscures the method of obscuration by citing its means as operating "in such manner as the light of the sun obscureth the light of the stars; which stars do no less exercise their virtue, by which they are visible, in the day than in the night." (*Leviathan* II)[14] Shame enhances the light of reason by projecting the cause of decay away from itself. The fresh, novel, vital, undegenerate, undecayed issuances of voice become potential pathogens. In the reversal of projection, the only voluntary use of the voice is to produce voluntary signs. The rest, stained by self-involvement with the shameful origin, belongs to the degeneracy of reason. Hobbes: "And words whereby we conceive nothing but the sound, are those we call absurd, insignificant, and nonsense." (*Leviathan* V)[15]

Through reversal, the least obscure becomes the most dim-witted, the least decayed the most decadent, and the least vital, the most voluntary. Similarly, the most vital is the least reasonable. The imagination's self-deception regarding the origin of voluntary signs must be preserved. The history of a progressive development of phonemic vocification is thereby served up. We have already noted the erasure surrounding the organic functionings of voice. Now we see, in Hobbes, how the meaning of the first quasi-signifying acts is obfuscated. After phonemes have been shaped into word-sounds but before denotation is scientifically fixed, metaphor and a more figurative way of speaking reign. In the history of spoken voice, metaphor stands nearer to the origin than unambiguous signification because its definitiveness is not yet distilled. It partially hides, partially specifies, the signified. Its usefulness with respect to phonemic domination is limited and suspect. Hobbes notes that metaphoric use involves deception. Although the deception that he speaks of is simply a nonliteralness (using words "in other sense than that they are ordained for"), what he points to is the revelatory role that metaphor has in the economy of desire. (*Leviathan* IV)[16] Metaphor speaks deceptively, not because it twists the truth, nor distorts the signifier-signified relation, nor skews the lines of denotation. It speaks deceptively because speech is deception. Born of cognitive shame, speech must swallow the discovery of its defect with every glottal stop. In its intention to lead away from literalness, metaphor threatens to force an acknowledgement on speech. In blurring the grid of reference, metaphor indicates the inchoate origin of speaking, the forcing of the imagination's will over the protesting cry of the organism.

In the knowledge of metaphor lies a twofold danger. Because metaphor practices deceit by intention, it promises to bring down the citadel of phonemic authority. Political deceit, keeping the discovery of shame from the light of reason, is viable only as long as subterfuge is a forbidden practice. Fear of punishment keeps the strict signifier-signified alignment from falling out of place. It also keeps persons from exploring the experience of vitality, the relation of cognition to sensation, and the wider capabilities of voice. The play of metaphor is an imposing threat to the work of referential security in the way that artistic freedom imperils fascism. How else can we understand the ardor of Hobbes's language when he says:

> Metaphors, and senseless and ambiguous words, are like *ignes fatui*; and reasoning upon them is wandering amongst innumerable absurdities; and their end, contention and sedition, or contempt? (*Leviathan* V)[17]

Metaphor spells a clear and present danger. Its exile is mandatory if the fragile economy of desire is to survive. Metaphor's potential defeat of cognition derives from its power to raise the awareness. Loosening the shackles of cognitive literacy, the figurative in speech allows room for the immediate, the sensory, the nonrepresentation, the organic element again to announce itself to human life. Consciousness first appears through vital motion and first disappears through the imagination. That is why a political state without metaphor is apt to be safe from consciousness. In metaphor is more than a trace of the origin of speech. The metaphor, as will be seen, is origin itself.

Metaphor is sedition to Hobbes's mind for a second reason. By his own admission, metaphorical speech is more originary than signification. The signifier-signified relation lies at the far end of progression from origin. Phonemic authority, the sovereignity of fear, the obscuration by imagination, the loss of sensory contact: all must be sufficiently developed in order for the sign to be sustained. Metaphor is an earlier stage of development, before the time when "the light of human minds is perspicuous words, but by exact definitions snuffed, and purged from ambiguity." (*Leviathan* V)[18] Metaphor is an incomplete transformation of the voice's cry, be it animal or human. Behind it the force of passion and sensate life is as yet unadulterated by the imagination. Though it practices deceit (which belongs to cognition), it also bears witness to the truth of human emotions and vitality. In its partial correspondence to what is true, spoken metaphor points beyond itself, back to the passions, shameless desire, and the voice's voice. Metaphor is thereby capable of revealing to Hobbes that which he necessarily conceals from himself—the metaphor of origin. The shift from a state of nature (war) to the polis (peace), from solitude to conversational society, from dispersion to union, from the anarchy of vital functionings to the sovereignty of mind is a metaphoric shift. The concealment of the nonliteral, unreasonable basis of history is the prime motivation for stressing both the fact of brutality and the brutality of fact prior to origin. The brute is the concealment of the lie.

What if Hobbes's thoughts concerning speech, which insist on signification, reference, definitiveness and the other cognitive virtues, in fact derive from the infamóus *ignes fatui*, the figurative and poetic dimension of word-sounds? If origin is a metaphor, a point having no strict denotation, then it is not subject to the law of identity. From a metaphor, both a thing and its opposite may be deduced. Thus Adam who received God's names received metaphors, that is, contradictories, not identities. The whole system of voluntary signs, based on the deceit which is metaphor, takes on a new meaning. So too his account of phonemic supremacy and pacification by the word-sound. Origin, that point when vocalic speaking pronounces itself victor over meaningless babble (the body), begins by effacing the speech of speaking. That is, it begins by effacing itself, rewriting the history of voice so that the phoneme is an advance, a positive progression, beyond inarticulate voicification. That which presents itself as the maker of origin, the creator of the originary metaphor, must remain concealed. The imagination must not know itself as imagination or else it would confront its secret shame. Hidden deception of self is the cause of its decadence. "This decaying sense," when turning inventive, invents in equivocal, metaphoric, and absurd terms. Its first, richest, and most primordial invention, the one most successful in leading itself away from its own dark truth, is the history of political society, its *arche* and its *telos*. The measure of success lies in the degree to which the originary myth deceives the deceiver.

The nature of metaphor is dangerous to Hobbes because it threatens to unmask his account of the progress of phonemic supremacy. History is necessarily progressive, a passage from the diversity of voice to the unity of spoken language, persons keeping company together, and the commonwealth. But history points back to a time prior to origin. In prehistory, need rather than desire gave people voice. And need is always diverse, different, dispersing. Prehistoric humanity

> being hereby forced to disperse themselves into several parts of the world, it must needs be that the diversity of tongues that now is,

proceeded by degrees from them, in such manner as need, the mother of all inventions, taught them; and in tract of time grew everywhere more copious. (*Leviathan* IV)[19]

People not bound by the shameful volition shamelessly give voice to the living conditions surrounding them. After the metaphorical point of origin, people progressively respond more and more in the coin of signification. But we must arrest the narrative at this point. Origin itself is invented by the inventor of signifying, the imagination, "this decaying sense." The originary metaphor, being the by-product of decay, gives the history of a decaying responsiveness to an environment soliticing vital response. It is a history of regression, of the refusal of humanity to accept the organic, sensory experience which answers the address of external bodies. Within this darker movement, the word-sound emerges as the regressive betrayal of people to a state of nature. The polis of denotation is ultimately an expression of shame over the betrayal of need by decadent desire. Origin is a convenient, metaphoric way of putting it.

From the metaphoric time of origin, the unspoken history of voice chronicles the degeneration of vocalic forces. Such dark bodings must be kept from the citizens of light. Hobbes bolsters his defense of the nobility of speech with the belated observation that good inventions can spring from degenerate minds. He says "that the longer the time is, after the sight or sense of any object, the weaker is the imagination." (*Leviathan* II)[20] Presumably, the intention is to say that the word-sound is far enough away from the tainted act of its invention itself not to be stained. The reasoning is a *non sequitor*. The activity of imagination may be weaker by the time that the signifer-signified replaces metaphor, which replaced the voice's voice. The entrenched habit, to the contrary, is more strongly established. Hobbes's error is one of metaphor: to conceive habit in the innocence of mechanism (movement "by springs and wheels as doth a watch") instead of the guile of the fox. Mechanical motion decays over time in the presence of resistance. The imagination, however, is self-willed and deceitful. It will do whatever necessary to protect its design. What it sets in motion, the lie, grows over time both in autonomy and extent. Referential speech is more deceptive than is metaphoric speech because it has ceased to make deception part of its practice. The direction in which the lie grows is lateral, away from the eye, away from the mind, toward what is already lost, decayed, ruined, and spoiled. Thus, the distance from imagination lessens the farther an act is removed from it. What amounts to the same thing, the imagination itself weakens as the lie grows. Liars require good memories ("imagination and memory are but one thing.") because of the rampant growth of self-deception. *(Ibid.)* Like a cancer, imagination weakens only because its colonies strengthen. The lie, when self-sustaining, is a second imagination, desirous of standing in the place of its inventor. It is even capable of believing that its creator has weakened and needs replacement.

Taking the origin as a point, distance equals weakness. Solitude, the spacing between humanity, is weakness as is diversity of vocalic sound production, the spacing between need. Yet at the same time the phoneme and the leviathan come into being only at a distance. Are they too born of weakness? They would be but for the economy of desire, shame. Hobbes says: "For the impression made by such things as we desire, or fear, is strong and permanent, for, if it cease for a time, of quick return: so strong it is sometimes as to hinder and break our sleep." *(Leviathan* III)[21] The strength that defeats the weakness of distance is the concealed "discovery of some defect of ability." That strength is not a positive but the malignancy of self-deception. The imagination in hiding causes the pressure of retention by virtue of its refusal to acknowledge that which it knows it lacks. The voice shaped by phonemic authority becomes a vehicle of retention. The spoken word provokes a tension in and closure of vital responsiveness. The precision, definitiveness, rigor, and strength of speech stem from its contractile effect on the organism. The initial equation (distance = weakness) is superceded of the invention of somatic tautness, of a turgor that passes for strength, and of a reactivity that masquerades as greatness. The initial defect is superceded by the defect of pretention.

In the originary metaphor, the brute's growl and the infant's babble are at once replaced successively by metaphor and by the spoken word. Although Hobbes lists metaphor as the sixth cause of absurd conclusions ("the use of metaphors, tropes, and other rhetorical figures, instead of words proper"), the difference of metaphor is its totality. *(Leviathan* V)[22] Within the metaphor, reality is metaphoric. Every element with which a metaphor plays is a metaphoreme. All contribute to the practiced deception that makes, in Hobbes's eyes, the metaphor anathema to education. In their context, metaphoremes enjoy a radical equality. None is more culpable in distorting the truth than any other. While some have more brilliance, none is more fictive, more invented, nor more artificial than any other. Within the originary metaphor, phonemic authority, the spoken word, and the signifier-signified relation are all metaphoremes. Each functions in the play which creates ambiguity, imprecision, and the fire of fatuity—so much feared by sovereign, citizen, and the author of the *Leviathan* alike. That the polity is a metaphor and not a precise denotation is fear-provoking since play, looseness, and unrestraint then assume new importance. That the body politic is hard and tensed, self-willed and martial in its rigor, becomes suspect. And that articulated sound requires a taut glottis and checked breath comes under question. Hobbes's choice of metaphor rather than theorem (like Spinoza) or treatise (like Aristotle) to tell the history of the commonwealth is a true act of imagination. Like a deceit, it is richer in possibilities than the mind that voices it.

Metaphor, unlike theorem or treatise, does not argue its truth. It exhibits it. Unlike cognition, it does not assume a position, define a resistance, and try to fend off opponents. More like the receptivity of vital motion, it embraces new rivals in the field as they present themselves. Not being attached to specific place, metaphor is inherently replaceable. Within the play of a single metaphor, metaphoremes move in and out of each other's position in the great war of contradiction. The grand reversals and great fluidity of Hobbes's history attest to its internal metaphoric movement. Obscuration, eclipse, distance, weakening are all phases of the same movement. Only Hobbes's blinding literalism and his hidden agenda of providing an apology for phonemic authority prevent him from carrying out a farther-reaching vocalic exploration. For, if the leviathan is a metaphor, it can be replaced in its metaphoremes or its entirety by a new metaphor. In the play of such a metaphor, we recover the vital substratum of the voice's voice wherein lies its freedom from phonemic domination.

What makes a metaphor ripe for replacement? Where decay is an operative force of an originary metaphor, the metaphoremes are sooner or later sapped of vitality. Shame, therefore, is a poor passion on which to base the conquest of voice by articulation. As we saw, the metaphor's practice of deception cannot, without loss, be directed against itself. Otherwise the secondary deceits vie to become replacements for the metaphor itself. Whether ingenuous or self-aware, the metaphor must play its deception away from itself, on the inquiring mind which needs to be prized of its rigidifying positions. An originary metaphor, for a start, must give a convincing account of the origin of metaphor. To make metaphor an impairment of "words proper" is again to throw the entire project of the originary metaphor into doubt. Hobbes's predispositions may lead him to neglect the obvious power of his choice of metaphor as method. They do not, however, interfere with the novel material which the metaphoremes turn up. Among them, he records for us the one successful revolt against phonemic authoritarianism:

> But all this language gotten and augmented by Adam and his posterity, was again lost at the Tower of Babel, when, by the hand of God, every man was stricken, for his rebellion, with an oblivion of his former language. (*Leviathan* IV)[23]

This single revolt of voice against articulatory forces throws the human sound-producing apparatus back to a beginning unencumbered by imagination, "this decaying sense." People thereat give voice to individual need, no longer restrained by the economics of desire. In the reborn childhood of humanity, the rebel's childhood, the sounds which voice makes, so fear-provoking to the established regime, are babblings. Reduced to infancy, at a time before the capacity to articulate is active, voice is babble. Hobbes's fear, inspired by the loss of phonemic control, hears voice as idiotic. For babble belongs not only to innocence but also to idiocy. The phonemic ambiguities of babble make it an inspiring direction for the further study of voice. Let me, with fresh ear, follow out this important indication, and turn to the infant's first voice (or the idiot's last), in hopes of discovering a metaphor fully adequate to the spoken and unspoken voicings of voice.

CHAPTER 6

BABBLE

Out of the mouth of babes and sucklings has thou ordained strength.
Psalms 8.2

Could speaking, the human articulation of meaning, be lacking in origin? Which would mean that the metaphor of origin, as given by Hobbes, does not apply to phonemic voicification. The arche-act of speaking, the "I" of speech, would in that case be antinomous. Kant's famous First Antinomy argues against applying the idea of origin to the world as a totality. Similarly the origin of speaking would be metaphorically unspeakable within the bounds of cognition. Or, what amounts to the same thing, any one metaphor (Hobbes's, for instance) would exhibit, within its metaphoremic reversals, flips, headstands, and pratfalls, the pageant of oppositions: progression, regression, weakening, strengthening, precision, ambiguity. It would also always be striving to encompass that point lying just before the originary beginning, the point when the voice, being unspoken, belongs to itself, the voice. We have seen that Hobbes's account behaves according to such a pattern. Does the metaphor of origin behave like an antinomy of reason?

The quick deduction is that speech lacks an origin. Because it is never at its source, it is always avoiding a return to a beginning, like the circumference avoids the empty center of a circle. Articulated voice, in that case, is like Io, wandering the Caucasus, pursued by the gadfly. But before we conclude the antinomous result, we need to become aware of the fuzziness surrounding the origin of metaphor itself. Hobbes's equation, metaphor = abuse of spoken voice, alerts us to the confused situation. Any power (cognition is one) expresses its conquest and need for domination by retelling history. The story that it spins replaces the older, subdued powers (gods, divinities, supreme forces) with aspects of itself and sets the time of battle back (after the necessary erasures) to zero. For instance, the Hebrew metaphor begins with Adonoi's fiat ("Let there be light!"), which calls to order the dark particles of prehistorical chaos. The conquered elements, while not lacking in voice, lack the adult means of offering a phonemically coherent account. From them, we are told nothing. From the Titans, we learn nothing not told through the speech of the Olympian pantheon. The situation in Hobbes is similar with respect to the imagination's originary insemination of the vital, bodily energies. The driving force behind a metaphor of origin is consolidation of the gains of violence. Though any account of metaphor's origin must be expunged, we have seen that the metaphoremes live a life of their own. In spawning the leviathan, metaphor plays a blurred, unexamined role, being an element of Titanic prehistory somehow entering into the birth of the word-sound. Metaphor is primitive absurdity which perpetually threatens speech with abuse. It predates the word proper but does not vanish entirely upon the latter's conquest of voice. Is contradiction unavoidable? Hobbes's project rests on the confusion between a metaphor of origin and the origin of metaphor. In the context of the first, the second remains a mystification. Understanding metaphor's beginnings—before its history is erased and reduced to an antagonism of speaking—allows us to move closer to the voice of voice.

Because of its secret violation, speaking carries with it the need to establish its origin. That is, it has need (though secretly) for metaphor, which need it must think abusive, degrading, and absurd. By contrast, no history of the origin of voice exists. Whereas speech, for Hobbes, is the God-given insemination of organic sensitivity by imagination, voice is "natural." Solitary humanity presumably gives voice to experience while in the state of war. As natural, voice exists in its repeated return to its origin and is never at a distance from its source without becoming other than the voice of voice. The naturalness of voice does not, however, imply its changelessness, its fixity, or its essentiality. Instead, voice expresses experience (as does dance, painting, or the culinary arts) by not annihilating the kinaesthetic matrix. Compare the distance of the phoneme which cleaves the organic from the cognitive. Distance is, in Hobbes's way of speaking, the "help of imagination." Through help, voice is relieved of a role in the history of human knowledge, is subtracted from that sum and from itself, until it is no longer heard. On its own behalf, voice, if heard, is originary without the addition of metaphor. It has no need for and is not helped by metaphor, a clever device of distance. Metaphor is an addition which is a subtraction of natural voice. To speech, however, metaphor is an addition which is an addition. Though of no help to voice, metaphor is supple enough to lead one back through speech to the organic vibration which is voice's voice. Thus, metaphor occupies the peculiar position, like a Platonic daemon, of relating to the absent member no matter which side of origin it happens to be.

The originary metaphor erases "nature" and introduces phonemic distance. Nature is a term appearing on one, the primordial, side of the equation inaugurating speech. From that point on, the natural is modified by articulation and ceases to exist. The natural, our voice's own origin, we know from our first beginnings. The voice of nature *(vox naturalis)* which initially suffers erasure is babble. Babble belongs to the infant, the idiot, to seizures of passion, and to cognition rendered incoherent. It is not so much the paradigm of natural voice but an attestation to its raw vital nativity. Babble is the body's sound-producing apparatus in operation without exterior directions. It stands on the brink of muteness which is the apparent vacancy of sound of the body's innermost processes. It is voice freed to voice but not freed to full humanity. Babble of passion, idiocy, intellectual short circuitry, anarthria, or senility is a feared aberration of sound-producing patterns. The apparent loss of the cognitive function excites our apprehensions of regression, madness, and death while the veil of uncommunicativeness turns us away from conversation and back to our ignorance of ourselves and our voice. One who babbles repeatedly requires institutionalization, incarceration, first aid, or sympathy for his or her defect or foible. An understanding of babble cannot get a foothold where our avoidance is so strong.

Infantile babbling, by contrast, does not offend our judgment, ostensibly presenting a form of purely natural voicification. Babble as it develops and fades in the very young child provides clues about the natural in voice.

The babbling voice is without distance from its voicing. Lacking distance, we are on the verge of recognition of voice. In the lack of distance, we are absent from the conversation which simultaneously keeps one person together with the other and away from oneself. That vacuity of comprehension, the rich moment of not knowing the subject and object of voice, calls an awareness of the voice-making being. The moment of my calling out in the dark woods startles me inasmuch as I do not recognize whose voice it is. A study must start thereat. The infant's babble becomes a stage before spoken history but in itself nothing. To abide in the absence is to turn understanding back from phonemic distance, cognition, and signification to the organism which speaks in babblings. Babble is the phonic expression of organic freeplay—which explains the difficulty we encounter in trying to imitate babble convincingly. Babble, the *vox naturalis*, returns us vocalically to ourselves as we are prior to the political act of phonemic insemination.

Babble seems to call us through metaphor to the origin which it is. But babble too has its precursor. Before it can babble, lallate, or coo, the infant cries. This fact does not make crying more "natural" than the naturalness of babble. To cry, for the infant, is to need. Need, the primordial economy which we saw supplanted in Hobbes by desire, is not necessarily a matter of distress or despair. Describing the crying infant, Rousseau says:

> He has only one language because he has, so to say, only one kind of discomfort. In the imperfect state of his sense organs he does not distinguish their several impressions; all ills produce one feeling of sorrow.[1]

To cry is to give voice to the absence which the infant feels vitally, be it hunger, warmth, or love. Filled, the infant babbles. Studies show that babble evolves from crying after the first postnatal month, but that crying continues developmentally to follow an independent course.[2] Phonemic authority introduces a distance which is an absence. Speech is grafted onto crying. Thus, Rousseau:

The first language of mankind, the most universal and vivid, in a word the only language man needed, before he had occasion to exert his eloquence to persuade assembled multitudes, was the simple cry of nature.[3]

Babble is left intact, having no "imperfection" from which to subtract a something. It is to be buried alive as desire replaces need. The fullness of organic freeplay remains a disturbing possibility in moments when distance collapses upon itself. The babbling idiot as the rebel.

Crying is no less natural than babble because it has an object (satisfying the need) while babble has none. Instead, both are global responses that voice offers to the immediate real. Both are voiced because each contrasts with normal (voiceless) breathing and with the vocal folds set in vibration by a moving column of air (and not open to allow the air to pass unimpeded). In both, the "natural" substratum of the retentive mechanism by which Aristotle instruments respiration and voicification already exists—as if prepared to receive its future cognitive conjugate. The natural is not disturbed by the retention of voicing in babble and crying because that retention belongs to the self-regulating and -maintaining mechanism of vital functioning. Retention becomes artificial, authoritarian, and preemptory only when an element foreign to the body intervenes to coopt power. Only when, that is, valuation shifts to conversation and the desire to imitate conversation. Jakobson gives careful attention to this fact. "Alongside the purposeless egocentric soliloquy of the child," he says,

> and gradually replacing this biologically oriented "tongue delirium" (to use Preyer's term) there arises and grows by degrees in children a desire for communication.[4]

The intrusive element is marked by the well-known impoverishment of human sound production after babbling. ". . . the phonemic poverty of the first linguistic stages . . . a kind of deflation."[5] The babbling infant with a rich phonetic repertory is replaced by a proto-speaker with a meager inventory. Jakobson explains:

> One can uniquely explain the *selection of sounds* during the transition from babbling to language from the fact of this transition itself, i.e., from the

new function of the sounds, through their becoming speech sounds, or more precisely from their *phonemic value*, which the sound thereby receives.[6]

Voice is deflated, acquires distance from a vocalic organic effulgence, and gains phonemic value in becoming speech. The matter of why phonemic value is valued is simple enough. Jakobson aligns himself closely with Hobbes. He says:

> Straightway these arbitrary sound-discriminations, occurring for the first time and based upon meaning, produce simple, meaningful, and stable sound oppositions, where are capable of being impressed on the memory, reproduced by desire and necessity and which become easy to remember.[7]

Mnemonic value, the instrumentality of desire, and the marshalling of organic perception make the phoneme a desirable advance over babbling. The babbler desires to imitate the "conceptual distribution of articulated sounds" of persons around him or her. But imitation inevitably means loss. Memory, like imagination, Hobbes tells us, operates on decaying sensitivity. It perpetuates the sense of decay which is distance through which filters all phonemic experience. The leap over the origin, away from "these arbitrary sound-discriminations," is the impetus into political society. Sound imitation is initiation into the commonwealth.

Babble presents us with sound in its organic play, before the workings of the articulatory components: voicing, nasality, place of articulation, and friction. The appearence of pulmonic-lingual consonants, plosives and dentals, and a great variety of vowel-like sounds marks the onset of the babbling period (three to ten months). To the politics of articulation, as to Hobbes, babbling reduces the means of production to zero. Babbling humanity is starved for phonemic sustenance, the stuff of conversation. Is it any wonder that Hobbes understands babble as retribution? Adult humanity is punished with babble (insanity, trauma, senility) for self-will, for its failure to acknowledge the origin of speech. Infant humanity likewise is punished with its love of pleasure in the absence of the phoneme. From the standpoint of articulation, phonic freeplay strips the infant of the manifold benefits of political conversation. In being not yet human, the infant is nonhuman. For the play that (as yet) avoids the work of commanding the organs of speech is the action of a creature imprisoned by its vital functionings. Infancy, for Hobbes, is retribution and imprisonment, a repetition of the fall at Babylon. In that condition, being and action, lacking rigor and retentiveness, are reduced to play. Strangely, play is closer to the primitive condition of war than is work. Opposites need not work at annihilating the other. Play suffices. As play, babble is a pleasure unto itself. The infant babbles for no reason other than the fact that free sound production is pleasing. One sound consumes, devours, and utterly destroys its predecessors. If we follow Hobbes, delight in punishment further signifies blame. Perversely, play is thereby deprived of its alliance with an originary metaphor. But in play, the organism as vocal instrument plays and is played upon pleasurably by forces belonging to a multileveled reality. This is the instrument before tuning and tempering; no stops exist. Sound is process rather than production. The organism sounds itself to explore the delights of the environment, internal and external. In its turn, it is sounded by what it contains and is contained by and is further delighted. Sound is continually in the process of being made, is perfectly imperfect, and reaches no end or finished point. Any one token of babbling, for this reason, is indistinguishable from another except by external means, time, place, or the like. Each sound is without existence until voiced and falls out of existence after the voice uncovers a new milieu. In its endlessness and endless novelty consists the enjoyment of free organic phonic expression. Joy is the arising, flourishing, and perishing *de novo* of *this* sound of the body. When articulation ceases to be a term waiting on the other side of the equation, the play of babble and the babble of play are no longer deprivations of a short-term prison. Babble babbles on.

I began questioning the applicability of the originary metaphor to voice's voice. Is there another? In its freedom, presence, self-delight, and unretained life, the infant's babble suggests a continuity of creation. Voice unbroken by the distance of the phoneme stands on neither one side of origin nor on the other. Origin provides no useful point of reference. Nothing stands behind, before, or beyond the babbling voice. That voice is always there. Inarticulate voice, in being immediately related to the body to which it gives sound, is given sound by it. The incomprehensible phonic strings are the body's sounding in the process of recreating its emergence from the complex of not yet unified organic happenings. If the play of the body's phonetic effulgences has design, it is to confer a proto-unity on the abundance of bodily occurrences. Babble induces proprioception, the body's specific awareness of itself. The body, the habitat of vital motion,

continually recreates the conditions of its own awareness, an awareness of the whole of the human being and an awareness of what is
greater than humanity. The sensitized soma, when receptive to a
relation with consciousness, incarnates a unity obscured by phonemic
distance. That unity alone is capable of responding to a reality far
surpassing human cognition. In babbling infancy, the absence (Hobbes:
a lack) allows an integral organic functioning which supports the
advent of consciousness. Babble is the annunciation of prioprocep-
tion. It phonically announces the help of a body awareness dissolved in
phonemic distance.

Babble is marked by the continuing emergence of novel phonic
events, both sounds which appear in the infant's environment and
ones which do not. What is erased when babble suffers erasure is the
uninterrupted emergence of voice. The spacing of distance implies
distance from origin. Distance repeatedly provokes the need to
account for nondistance, immediacy, and contact. The metaphor of
origin therein replaces that of continuous creation. Privation replaces
fullness, blameworthiness replaces innocence, work takes the place of
play, and need (followed by desire) supplants plenty. The integration
of functioning under the influence of an unknowing consciousness is
rendered obsolete by the regulation of a knowing mind. The integrat-
ing power of voice (babble) is cast aside while its dis-integrating efficacy
(speech) is cultivated. The (political) view that babble is proto-speech,
learned by imitation, is, moreover, vitiated by the experience of deaf
infants who babble normally. What in babble serves to allow a
momentary equilibrium in the disparate functionings is effaced in
both types. The phonemic virtues, as Jakobson puts it, "capable of
being impressed on the memory, reproduced by desire and necessity
and which become easy to remember," are thereby installed as
sovereign.

When we extract the metaphoric content, continuous creation
gives us a new baseline through which to uncover the voice of voice.
Babble is a point on it, not of origin (as where, for example, the axes of
vitality and imagination might intersect) but of the emergence of a
pattern of human vocalic capability which recurs at other points. The
reappearance of babbling in adult life, when stripped of its pathological overtones, means that the pattern is not extinguished by
phonemic authority without a trace. In adult babble recreation of the
harmony of infantile awareness is not often achieved. Disrepair of
functionings, self-deception, overreliance on cognition, and entrenched
fear are reasons why the later return to babbling fails to renew the

human condition. If we enlarge the focus on the babbling infant and include the body's movements, we find another point to which the metaphor of continuous creation applies. The motor expression of organic free play, the gesture, shares many of the nonoriginary features of babble: directness, spontaneity, self-sufficiency, and inarticulateness. Expressing the motility of the organism, it re-balances the separate functionings and recreates conditions of body awareness. Unbound by phonemic distance, it permits the organic sensitivity to move outward and reestablish the relation between sensation and the surrounding environment. The emergence of one gesturing from another proceeds by the rules of play rather than by an exterior model. Though nonvocalic, the gesture enjoys a mysterious relation to the voice, apparent at one extreme in the gestures of a babbling infant and at the other in the actor's gestures in dramatic theatre. Can gesture allow the identity of the voice's voice further to show forth?

The expressivity of gesture as motile free play sometimes serves the originary metaphor. In this capacity, gesture is the root on which to graft the trunk of spoken voice, speech. Gesturing becomes the habitual accompaniment to learned predispositions of the articulatory organs. Its freedom is semiotically yoked by its signifying function. It is secondary speech, speech stripped of voice, a physical mutism which permits us to know what the gesturer is "really saying." The view that gesture is an intact, primitive system of signification, ready to be coopted by spoken voice, is Condillac's. Let me turn to his thought. His account of origin pictures two children shipwrecked after the deluge. Like Hobbes, Condillac's conversation begins with archaic fear and despair. Unlike Hobbes, gesture bridges the gap between passion and phonemic distance. Condillac tells us that the two children's

> mutual converse made them connect with the cries of each passion, the perceptions which they naturally signified. They generally accompanied them with some motion, gesture or action, whole expression as yet of a more sensible nature. (*Essay*, II.I.2)[8]

Primitive, i.e., voiceless, speech is the language of need as yet unmodified by the distance of cognition. It is instinctive response turned toward mutual aid. Persons "by instinct alone . . . asked and gave each other assistance. I say *by instinct alone*; for as yet there was no room for reflexion." (Ibid.) Instinct for Condillac lives in a confused, unformed state. Instinct is bodily but only insofar as the body suffers feelings. The body is the mobile face of what one lacks and feels in the absence of. It is the articulatory organ of affective, not organic, expression. It is not the body's body, but the emotions' body.

Although gesture for Condillac is the ancestor of speech, speech makes the history. His interest in the hegemony of spoken voice projects the same reversals onto bare gesturing as does Hobbes onto voice. Gesture (like voice) exists only to prepare the ground for speech. It has no independent reason for being. In that respect, gesture is voiceless voice, a subtraction to which the phoneme must be added in order to have a positive sum. Condillac:

> Speech succeeding the language of action, retained its character. This new method of communicating our thoughts could not be contrived without imitating the first. (II.I.I.13)[9]

As with Hobbes, the invention of the phoneme "the most noble and profitable" serves vocalically to signify the mute cognitive significance of interior monologue. Speech imitates gesture only because the latter embodies the signifer-signified relation in action. Once people "had acquired the habit of connecting some ideas with arbitrary signs, the natural cries served them for a pattern, to frame a new language." (II.I.I.6)[10] In the logic of replacement, the next step is simple: "In order then to supply the place of the violent contortions of the body, the voice was raised and depressed by very sensible intervals." Stress, accent, and intonation complete the transition from one system to the next. The manifold qualities of human sound production supplant rudimentary gestures, or rather, are the living fossils of gesturing, voicified and civilized. The gesture disappears into the monotony of spoken speech as the occasional pique of emotion; "different emotions are signified by the same sound varied in different tones." Condillac:

> Ah, for instance, according to the different manner in which it is pronounced, expresses admiration, pain, pleasure, sadness, joy, fear, dislike, and almost all the passions. (II.I.II.13)[11]

The primary reason why gesture is proto-speech is not because it gives the signs of feeling. "Men begin to speak the language of gesture," Condillac says in his *Logic*, "as soon as they feel, and then they speak it without intending to communicate their thoughts." (*Logic*, II.2)[12] True, gesture is symbolic passion. Gesture is proto-speech, however, primarily because it substitutes passion for motile

play, feeling for organic sensation. Only because gesture comprises
this elemental replacement can it be replaced by the phoneme. The
primordial inadequation of gesture, as exemplified in the two children's speaking by action, lies precisely in the substitution of passion
for vital motion. From the initial displacement of organic sensitivity,
Condillac's whole history follows. As cognition gradually takes over
the reins of speaking by action, passions inevitably cool. The decrease
in inflected sound variation follows the increased need of referential
precision, "what those men wanted, who first invented the use of
speech." (II.I.II.13)[13] The dampening of the native expansiveness of
gesture gives testimony to a progress:

> If we are satisfied with a slight variation of the voice, it is because the
> mind has been sufficiently enlarged and improved by the great number
> of ideas which we have acquired, and by the habit we have formed of
> connecting them with sounds.[14]

Speaking by action gives way to spoken voice because it is passionate,
inherently deficient, and in itself represents an absence whose place
must be filled by the distance of phonemic authority. The deficiency
marks a recurrent failing of Condillac. He does not take the root of
gesture, the organic need (instinct) of the arche-speakers, as seriously
as its first replacement, passion: "the cries of the passions contributed
to enlarge the operations of the mind, by giving occasion naturally to
the mode of speaking by action." (II.I.I.5)[15] The lack reflects his
favoring the infant's cry (passion) over its babble (fullness) as the root
of gesture. Necessity rather than delight becomes the medium of
speech.

When gesture is the cry of passion, it belongs to the inferior and
inadequate in speaking. As speech matures and passions cool, feeling
occupies a more subjective, internal position. Emotion has only
opaque reference by means of imprecise, nondenotative means.
Feeling, though a mode of speaking predating the phoneme, resists
the chilling embrace of speech. Though pliant, feeling lacks sub-
missiveness. Passion's lack of receptiveness to signification explains
why only figurative or metaphorical meaning is given by spoken voice.
"For example," Condillac writes in "Of the origin of poetry,"

> in the mode of speaking by action, to give an idea of a person that had
> been frightened, they [the primitives] had no other way than to mimic
> the cries and natural signs of fear . . . . A single word, which depicts

nothing, would not have been sufficiently expressive to have immediately succeeded the mode of speaking by action. (II.I.VII.66)[16]

Condillac rectifies a shortcoming of Hobbes by making all of speech a metaphor.

Metaphor is speech at a loss over the inexpressibility of passion. It is speech whose cross is to bear the defectiveness of signifying the life of feeling. Although it properly expresses the passion, it only gives expression to a defect. As with Hobbes, so with Condillac: the voice, arrested by an emotion, trips and stammers. The phonemic translation of that voice in images and figures, therefore, repeats the inarticulate movements of the tongue. If the phonemic imitates the gesturing cry of passion, the result will be necessarily poor. Metaphor is that second-class citizenship. Thus, all of speech.

Impoverishment by inexactitude, loss of designation, inferiority in expression: these constitute reasons for the banishment of metaphor and what it figures—passion—from articulated voice. Yet metaphor has a Napoleonic resilence; it repeatedly reappears from exile to show its face in the homeland. The repetition of metaphor in language reiterates the sentence together with the impossibility of carrying it out. In metaphor, speech stumbles over the defect which phonemic distance tries to remedy and like a weak sicknurse catches the contagion instead. How can feeling be erased from conversation? The metaphor sticks to speech like glue, the ego's unwanted property which stubbornly refuses to be thrown away. "When mankind had once acquired the art of communicating their conceptions by sounds," Condillac writes,

> they began to feel the necessity of inventing new signs proper for perpetuating them, and for making them known at a distance. Their imaginations then represented nothing more to them than those same images, which they had already expressed by gestures and words, and which from the very beginning had rendered language figurative and metaphorical. (II.I.13.127)[17]

Passion's imagistic elusiveness continues to recapitulate the attempt to make gesticulation significatory. In conversation, metaphor does not remain silent for long. The aliveness of metaphor is at once a measure of the life of signification and its death. It means that human need cannot be directly stated but that indirect statement suffices. Put another way, in spoken voice attention must (by the logic of distance) be taken away from the emotions. Thus only a derived attention is available to feeling. Even this solution is not final. Our life of conversation, the life of truncated emotions, continues to be threatened by the original avertedness, for figures and metaphors "have been the first and principal cause of the decline of languages." (II.I.XIV.141)[18]

Gesture, the promise of sounding voice from a new basis, in terms of a new metaphor, shows itself in Condillac to be thoroughly infected by phonemic authority. Not the gesture of plenitude but need, not the body's gesture but the passions', gesture reduces itself to the absence of reference. The single case that Condillac allows the pure presence of the organism to stand forth gesturally is dance. Dance gestures without the cry of passion which already represents a distance from motile free play. Dance thus "acted upon the imagination with greater force, the impression was more durable." Furthermore, "its expression contained even something elevated and noble, which the language of articulate sounds, as yet poor and barren, could not come up to.[19] (II.I.I.11) Condillac might have added, *or could ever come up to.* As soon as a speaking by acting becomes the organ of passions, its expressivity is bent, deficient, replaceable, false. Dance succeeds in expressing the body's motility by not rerecording the sensational in terms of the affective. Its life is that of vital motion. It is animated proprioceptively. It is the bodily enactment of continuous creation. Hence, dance metaphorically presents us with that face. The content of expression is therein conveyed without distance to another's sensitivity. That content, a state of consciousness (as opposed to the consciousness of a state), acts "with greater force" than any phonemic transcription because the impression is not broken by interval, cognition, memory, or self-deception. One organic unity transmits consciousness of itself and of a higher unity ("something elevated and noble") to which it is gesturally related.

Dance, in its choreography of improvisation, alone adds nothing to gesture. It allows motility to express the pure presence of the organism. Dance of course is unvoiced, voiceless. Grafting speaking by action onto dance is not, however, vitiated for Condillac by the silence of dance but by its elevation. He tells us intriguingly that "David danced before the ark" in order to communicate with God.[20] Gesture, voice, and speech are of interest only insofar as they conform to the ontology of absence. Dance inherits a presence derived from ontological plenitude, from an organic wholeness which stands in direct relation to a consciousness supportive of human consciousness.

Dance, therefore, falls outside of fragmented humanity, divided within itself, self-willed, and self-defeated. "Whenever therefore I happen to say," Condillac warns us,

> *that we have no ideas but what come from the senses*, it must be remembered, that I speak only of the state into which we are fallen by sin. This proposition applied to the soul before the fall, or after its separation from the body, would be absolutely false. (I.I.I.8)[21]

The gesture that can be spoken of belongs to the economy of dispersion, the fallenness of cognition, the sins of the marriage bed after the imagination inflicts its secret shame. That gesture is closed. Its closure, together with closing out the voice of voice, is guaranteed by the body's closure, the soul's closure, and their dysrelation which permits only closed attitudes, unpleasant emotions, and ideas cleaved on their informing organic life. In a word, Condillac's closure substitutes muteness for the open register of babble.

CHAPTER 7

CHANT/SONG

With the great gift of speech, an unknown something is stolen from voice. I have tried to locate the loss by listening to history, the storehouse of all loss. In speaking, the voice's voice is throttled. The spoken voice thus diminishes our humanity. I am concerned with finding an effective understanding of recovery. My question has focussed on the equation, speaking = *vox naturalis* plus x. By the law of identity, this becomes, *vox naturalis* = speaking minus x. The metaphor of origin attempts to assign a value to the unknown variable. Any value, be it articulatory imitation or gesture, encompasses the political act which establishes the hegemony of the phoneme. The metaphor of origin, the equation, is unswervingly directed toward that one end, a state of phonemic authority. Yet due to the imperfect status that the metaphor accords itself as metaphoric, its behaviour is obsessively deluded. As a gloss on gesture, passion, or primitive sound imitation, metaphor is a possible substitute for x, the unknown additive to natural voice. The equation, however, has no possible solution. Its undecidability has led me to question the meaning of metaphor, gesture, and the *arche* of speech, and to suggest that a new metaphor, continuous creation, elucidates voice's voice in a more satisfactory fashion. Continuous creation attempts neither addition to nor sub- traction from the proprioceptive data which voice's voice defines. Babble supplies us with the phenomenon of voice in process of creation.

I want to explore an independent approach to voicing. But first, we need to dispel any residual hopes for revealing the *vox naturalis* in passion, one proposed value for *x*. In an influential passage, Merleau- Ponty seeks, after Condillac's example, to locate in the feelings the term missing between phonemic voice and voice's voice. The phoneme (as in the Hobbes-Saussurean view) is not merely the arbitrary authority instituting political control over the naive, vital, kin- aesthetic subject. Now the word-sound rules with the voice of emotion. "If we consider only the conceptual and delimiting meaning of words," Merleau-Ponty says,

> it is true that the verbal form . . . appears arbitary, but it would not longer appear so if we took into account the emotional content of the word, which we have called above its "gestural" sense.[1]

Passion herein assumes a new role. It mitigates the violence of phonemic domination by reiterating in sound what is already pri- mordially felt. Violence takes on the positive value of emotional self- recognition. Never mind that gesture is collapsed into passion without a residue, or that the proprioceptive energy of voice is swept away in the fit of feeling. We are returned to the originary economy which is passion. Among the passions is ardent competition for what is available in small supply—the attention. The currency of exchange is need. Need arouses the attention, momentarily capturing it, and therewith activates the body, irrespective of the body's awareness, in order to secure the object.

Merleau-Ponty continues his moderate defense of the politics of domination:

> It would then be found that the words, vowels and phonemes are so many ways of "singing" the world, and that their function is to represent things not, as the naive onomatopoeic theory had it, by reason of objective resemblance, but because they extract, and literally express, their emotional essence . . . . The predominance of vowels in one

language, or of consonants in another, and constructional and syntactical systems, do not represent so many arbitrary conventions for the
expression of one and the same idea, but several ways for the human
body to sing the world's praises and in the last resort to live it.[2]

Affectivity comes into primordial predominance because the emotions continually react to events and objects. These reflexes of the life
of the feelings leap out at the world with such force and certainty that
we ascribe an objective value to them. Certainly the child does. The
conviction is that the world wears the happy (or sorrowful) face, not
the emotions themselves. The belief that the feelings correspond
somehow to the "emotional essence" of things, as seen above,
indicates the projective operation of cognition. What could be clearer
than to say, "We need, then, to seek the first attempts at language in
the emotional gesticulation whereby man superimposes on the given
world the world according to man?"[3] In Merleau-Ponty's case, the
reactive state of feeling effaces the *tabula rasa* of body awareness just as
need effaces plenitude. The emotional charge takes precedence over
the equilibrium of organic perceptiveness and takes charge of the
body. Motor reflexes are organized for the leap to action, to speaking
by action, and to speaking, period. The initial effacement does not,
however, disappear without an erased history: that the world is the
way that one feels it to be is the fundamental theorem of the reactive
emotions. Attention to the basal proprioceptive condition of our
humanity is totally submerged in the inflated life of feeling. From this
inattention arises the voice. The song sung of "the world's praises" is
the halleluja of passion's victory. The unsung victim is the body.

Speaking by action, for Merleau-Ponty, occurs first in song, not
the body's unvoiced gesturing (Condillac). Put another way, "emotional gesticulation" is not gesture plus voice but an unspecified
entity, the sung voice. Merleau-Ponty thus arrives at an intermediate
solution for the unknown variable x in the equation of originary
speech—song. Sung voice is not an addition because it already
involves a difference, the subtraction of the voice of body awareness.
The difference, Merleau-Ponty acknowledges, effaces the *vox naturalis*.
The natural vocalic response, uncommandeered by passion or cognition, does not even belong to human prehistory:

> It is no more natural, and no less conventional, to shout in anger or to
> kiss in love than to call a table "a table." Feelings and pasional conduct
> are invented like words.[4]

Once the vocal genius of sung voice, the vocal apparatus placed at the disposal of feeling, is the arche of speech, the series of oppositions, natural-conventional, voluntary-arbitrary, innate-learned, vital-cognitive, ceases to apply because of the intrinsic ambiguity of emotional need. In that economy, both a thing and its contradictory serves to satisfy a passion. One's fear of power is at the same time a love for it, one's aversion to a person is an attraction to him or her. The fundamental equivocity of feeling resounds in all voice, sung, spoken, declaimed, prerecorded. In driving the beginning of voice back to the passionate insurrection which conceals an ever-present body awareness, Merleau-Ponty makes a free-floating, chaotic melange definitive of all vocal, all human, endeavors. "Everything," he says,

> is both manufactured and natural in man, as it were, in the sense that there is not a word, not a form of behaviour which does not owe something to purely biological being—and which at the same time does not elude the simplicity of animal life, and cause forms of vital behaviour to deviate from their pre-ordained direction through a sort of *leakage* and through a genius for ambiguity which might serve to define man.[5]

Wallowing in the primeval muck of the feelings, sung voice is incapable of clarifying its position in the war of opposites. Each opposite clings with equal strength. Voice is thereby deprived at the beginning of knowing itself. Self-recognition never belongs to voice. What amounts to the same thing, voice must remain stupid and stupified. Which is to say, mute. Merleau-Ponty conjures anew the spectre of a mutism.

Sung voice has recourse to itself only through metaphor. Metaphor for Merleau-Ponty (as for Condillac and Hobbes) preserves ambiguity by bolstering the inadequate and inferior in place of the elevated in speech. Unlike Condillac and Hobbes, Merleau-Ponty's metaphor is an addition to voice posterior to the point of its beginning. Whereas the earlier thinkers relegate metaphor to brute or primitive humanity, beings in the dawn of their becoming, Merleau-Ponty discovers in metaphor the mysterious additive which dislocates forever the natural in voice. Not literalness or denotation but metaphor irreversibly transmutes the proprioceptive content of sound production into the other, phonemically charged, figuratively inclined voice. This is passion's voice thinly disguised:

> A contraction of the throat, a sibilant emission of air between the tongue and teeth, a certain way of bringing the body into play suddenly allows itself to be invested with a *figurative significance* which is conveyed outside us.[6]

Hobbes and Condillac give metaphor a place just past the fall from an integral state of consciousness, as if the figure or surd still bore a faint impression of voice's voice. That impress must be eradicated for voice to become a good spokesperson. Yet in metaphor is hope, progress, and amelioration in its transient appearance in human history. Metaphor partially partakes of the ontology of absence from which history, phonemic domination, and thought arise, and partially of the older, chthonic ontology of presence. Merleau-Ponty, however, seizes on metaphor as miraculously creating spoken voice from its own ambiguity: "For the miracle to come about, phonetic 'gesticulation' must use an alphabet of already acquired meanings, the word-gesture must be performed in a certain setting common to the speakers."[7] The miracle is not, therefore, that "figurative significance" causes the resurrection of the hidden human awareness (that belongs to proprioception). It is that we acquire through imitation the fallen condition of our voice. Metaphor is the permanent content of history, not a passing epoch. Moment by moment, "under a fresh law unknown to the subject or to the external witness," our voice is shaped by common metaphor into a sound in which it no longer recognizes its nature. Not to be replaced by a transcendent system of reference, metaphor eternally recapitulates the distance from ourselves which we suffer and live. No hope exists to move "beyond" metaphor. Metaphor, a mythical creature, half-thing, half-nothing, a hybrid which earlier thinkers sought to slew, is accorded by Merleau-Ponty the full power of human voice. Voicing, sung, unsung, spoken, or otherwise, becomes metaphor, the figure extended by the broken, fractionated, believer in the God-givenness of the fallen state.

Sung voice is "emotional gesticulation." Its character is essentially elegiac, a paean to the human prison, humanity kept from the possibility of becoming itself. The peculiar strength of attraction between vocal song, the voice musically inflected and modulated, and affective life reveals in denial the erased term. Intonation, rhythm, tempo, and melody make audible the global vibration which is our organic sensitivity. In the fate and destiny of that subhuman attraction, already obvious in Merleau-Ponty, is contained (as the positive is photographically contained in the negative) the moving song of the body. The transposition of mask for physiogomy and the lifting of passion's veil at the same time disclose the erotic basis of the union. Plato informs us of certain habits of eros. When the erotic predominates, desire goes in quest of permanence and immortality. The neediness of eros lies in the search for eternal life. In passion's sirenic song, its attempt to extract the "emotional essence" of things,

voice is dislocated. From its function of making heard the proprioceptive and its relation to human and suprahuman consciousness, it
reframes in musical articulation passion's short-lived existence.
Musical expression lends immortality to the sorrow, anger, joy, or
fear which perishes in a flash. That which outlives death itself, the
song which never dies, the note that lasts forever, is the signifier, now
musically endowed. Song, the erotic conquest of the organs of voice
by passion, has by backward entry become spoken voice.

The erotic appeal of sung voice stems from the fantasy of a
heaven in which everything is closed and always the same. This is the
internal song played for the mind alone. We saw above its hidden
operation in unsung voice. By the technology of deferred attention,
the intellect is able continually to escape the presence of the world and
to inhabit the eternity of the sign. Like deferred interest, the debt
need not be paid until the mind retires from the scene, at breakdown,
senility, or death. The inner song soothes and entertains the "savage
beast" prone to respond to the sting of reality. The emotions, which
normally provide an independent ground partaking of neither the
mentally changeless nor the physically contingent, are intellectualized
by an ironic Spinozan twist. Feelings which arise and perish in the
blink of an eye now persist in the prodigious repeatability of sung
voice. They themselves play the register of the voice singing sounds.
They are the singer. Song is the vocal alphabet, the inflected
phoneme, of passion. The hegemony of musical articulation, which
preceeds by one the Hobbes-Saussurean polis, is the product of erotic
distraction. It subverts nonvocal, unmusical humanity with the
vindictiveness of a distraught lover. That sung voice gains an
autonomy and turns against the person is the danger of inflation,
intoxication, and sensuality. An Apollonian firmament ceases to
appeal to the Dionysian; the Maenads in the end destroy Orphic song.
Eros, however, calculates only how to gratify desire. In the calculus
danger is always minimalized.

The reductive resonance of all human functionings to a single
one brings us back to the politics of repression. Voice reduced to
mechanics strips us of vocally contacting the awareness at the heart of
ourselves. Herbert Spencer's analysis of sung voice gives a good
example. He says:

> Thus we find all the leading vocal phenomena to have a physiological
> basis. They are so many manifestations of the general law that feeling is
> a stimulus to muscular action .... The expressiveness of these various

modifications of voice is therefore innate . . . . When the like sound is made by another, we ascribe the like feeling to him; and by a further consequence . . . have a certain degree of it aroused in ourselves.[8]

We can glimpse another operation of the metaphor of origin: reductive repression. The song of voice is eliminated along with the voice of voice. When we return to Condillac, the erasure is also apparent. He tells us:

At the origin of languages the manner of pronouncing admitted of inflexions that were so distinct, as a musician might prick it down, making only some small changes; I shall say then that it partook of the nature of music. (II.I.II.14)[9]

What is Condillac's proof that "words, vowels and phonemes are so many ways of 'singing' the world?" It consists in the work of enumerating types of inflexions, determining their motivating passions, and correlating them with elements of the phonemic system. That work places song as the basis of a physiology of passion. Knowing the body's reaction to the phonemic command of passion gives us complete knowledge of song.

Let us try to follow the reduction process as I have just outlined it in Condillac. In the beginning, "the natural cries necessarily introduce the use of violent inflexions; since different emotions are signified by the same sound varied in different tones." (II.I.II.13)[10] The primordial cry, a cry of need, is naturally signifying and naturally song. The need itself obliges the voiced cry to be song, to be sung speech. For we moderns, unlike the first people, need no inflection. "If we are satisfied," Condillac tells us,

with a slight variation of the voice, it is because the mind has been sufficiently enlarged and improved by the great number of ideas which we have acquired, and by the habit we have formed of connecting them with sounds.[11]

Primitive humanity by contrast lives in poverty of signifiers. This impoverishment is stronger than natural need since it determines what is to follow—history, speech, and polity—more than the other. Intonation, the voice "raised and depressed by very sensible intervals," becomes the first product of the inaugural economy. Intoned voice is not, however, a desired invention since desire is already at the disposal of cognitive aspiration. Intoned voice is fathered by necessity, is not willingly or caringly brought into existence, is not the hoped-for favorite—spoken voice—"what those men wanted, who first invented the use of speech."[12] Intoning in voice needfully makes do with an inferior means of signification, the way one does in a foreign country when not speaking the language. Intonation itself is infected by the lack of paternal love, a stoical love that favors suppressed emotional expression and is overly sensitive to the primordial violence enacted on the body. Intonation issues from the callow son who has not yet acquired the manly virtues of reframing feeling in terms of referential indirectness.

The cadences of song are born into the world to suffer a lack of phonemic value. The unwanted son, song, is abandoned to the paleolithic forests as soon as words are sired. Condillac tells us:

> At the origin of languages, mankind meeting with too great a difficulty in devising new words, had no other means for a long time of expressing the emotions of the soul, than the natural cries, to which they gave the character of instituted signs.[13]

Need over time strengthens cognition, moving it away from mimesis into phonemic invention, strictly speaking. Hence, in most tongues, intonation yields to the multiplication of words. Where it does not, for example, the Chinese use of tonality, evidence points to a yet enfeebled seed, the absence of "a more fruitful imagination." (II.I.II.15)[14] The progress of history, however, strips speaking of the effeminate play of tones and their hyperactive effect on feelings. The orphaned son, song, is no longer allowed to commune with spoken voice, "prosody." The articulated line is flattened, regularized, grammaticized, and declaimed while song is left to survive with the artifacts (musical instruments) of the woods.

Still, the mind's enchantment by song keeps it in the spoken domain long after cognition acquires its potent phonemic seed. Condillac regards the voice under the spell of tone as a weakling, desireless and effete. He thus prepares the way for the extinction of intonation: "Established customs oftentimes subsist even when the wants which gave rise to them are at an end."[15] But the voice in song was never wanted, was a displacement of voice not authorized by cognition but by necessity. Hence, its persistence, the persistence of raw, unintellectualized emotion, is the action of a semi-autonomous fixation or obsession. Sung voice is the barbarism of voice, voice's savage rites, which survives side by side with prosody. Its is the persistence of a fantasy which, being unwanted, desires to be heard. Long after cognition has stopped entertaining intonation as a significatory device and finds it offensive—as "when we think a comedian overacts his part"—intonation continues to steal denotative meaning from voice.[16] (II.I.III.16) Classical languages, Greek and Latin, tend to like the undesirable aspect of voice. Did we not see that intonation "which at that time was looked upon as natural in familiar discourse, partook so much of the nature of chant or song, that it was impossible for them [the speakers] to imagine such a medium as our manner of declaiming?"[17] Habituation enfeebles the very constitution of spoken voice. Use becomes an infatuation with the inferior in speech and promises more of the same. It occasions the resurgence of the forbidden, nonphonemic element. This is the song under its own unsignifying power. To wit, accent—"which independently of the meaning of a word, or of an entire phrase, determined the voice to fall on certain syllables and to rise on others."[18] (II.I.III.17) Accent or the rhythmic life of sung voice is enchanting because it is chant. Its spell moves us vitally. Chant is that vital motion, the organic pulse of life, ever-changing yet repetitive, with which body-awareness vibrates. Accent in voice is the other. It defies signification because of its fullness of presence. If voice admits of accent, it has already opened itself to the recognition of the unwanted son, the song which is wild, raw, unwanted, unintellectual. Such voice is capable of alliances with a totally human consciousness and with a consciousness which being other supports humanity. The existence of accent in classical languages exposes the contradiction whose birth is song for Condillac:

> How those accents never happened to clash with the expression, there is only one way of accounting. We must absolutely suppose, that according to the pronunciation of the ancients, the inflexions expressive of the thought, were so often and so sensibly varied, that they could not clash with those required by the accents. (II.I.III.17)[19]

Only the flimsiest preestablished harmony keeps voice on its phonemic course. Only when vocal song (accent) is isolated from spoken voice, and passion's inflection conveniently detached from signification, can conflict be avoided. Such is Condillac's course. In voice, chant is only a chance appearance.

In sung voice, the nonsignifying other appears first as intonation and accent, then of rhythm. Modulation and movement are equally natural and undesired. Desire has the unnatural as object, a monotone. "People accustomed to conduct their voice by distinct intervals, would find our pronounciation to be a lifeless monotony."[20] Desire for speech, originary desire which haplessly creates song, is the inverse of desire for inflection. Yet Condillac calls on one of the inverted terms, nature, to explain vocalic rhythm. "It was not therefore natural," Condillac says,

> that a people, whose prosody was in some measure musical, should observe equal stops in each syllable: this method of pronouncing would not have sufficiently imitated the mode of speaking by action. (II.I.III.25)[21]

Modulation and movement in the body's gesturing, as it actuates desire, are copied into voice's gesturing. What moves the voice, lending song its percussive qualities and creating the voiced interval, cannot be desire, a groping after the nonnatural, the fantastic, the unreal—in short, the monotone. Instead, it must be the undesired, the undesirable, the plenitude which out of fulness does not have the manly virtue of need to seek out the object. The natural and undesired, the weakly brother who sings in voice, is proprioception, the integral body awareness whose lack is nonexistent and whose nonexistence is the hidden cause of phonemic desire.

The polarities of Condillac's analysis of song thus become clearly audible. Desire, passion, need (the unnatural) impel people toward quality in voice: the phonemic contour which recontours the organs of the body as well as the body's awareness of the real. The *telos* is monotonality, monotony, and monologue. The unintended and undesired creation initially is song, the voice as it is in the wholeness of its own nature. The sung voice introduces quantity, "the sensible difference between long and short syllables."[22] Quantity in voice transmits the basal vibration of the body, calling an awareness of its condition and the condition of the world surrounding. Its *telos* is activation, address, and embodiment. Quantity demands spontaneous response, quality demands repetitious gratification. Tempo and rhythm, movement and modulation, then threaten the erotic acquisitiveness essential to phonemic character. Wanting nothing, they enfeeble the passions and the perceptive organs which the emotions control. Being natural, they gravitate toward the equilibrated state, fullness of being, contentment, and presence. How does Condillac describe their polar combination in sung voice? A fortuitous harmony veils the conflict. "Quantity, and pronouncing by distinct intervals, have kept pace together, and altered very nearly in the same proportion." (II.I.III.15)[23] Harmony, the articulated voice of reason and desire, quietens the rupture of song by pronouncing an aesthetic.

Aesthetics functions to train voice to the monotone. True, the interval between phonemic units is unavoidable. It is, moreover, a perilous fact. It should not call attention to the basal current, the quantity of percussing energy, from which it stems. That discovery could lead to a reversal of the reversal which desire has engineered. Theatrical song is the case in point. Ancient performance in its cathartic and organic dimensions "would deviate too widely from our manner of pronouncing, ever to seem natural to us." (II.I.III.26)[24] Sung voice's power to restore incarnate awareness is not only nonnatural but unaesthetic. The artificial modulations and movements appeal to the aesthetic sense which has replaced the natural. Condillac says, regarding his contemporary French public performance:

> We were sensible it could not be brought near enough to our ordinary pronounciation; we chose therefore to heighten it with music, in order to indemnify us by its artificial charms, not indeed for the loss of any natural beauty, but of a habit which we took for such. (II.I.III.28)[25]

Sung voice, quantity in voice, tempo and rhythm, all serve to embellish the sign. With the habituation of desire, the peril of the song's song bursting forth is finally defused. Preference is for artifice. It reflects the power of its inventor, cognitive imagination. The interval between phonemes, whose necessity was the possible upsurge of the undesired, itself only adds to the beauty of speech—the way a speech defect makes the audience more attentive to what is said. Condillac's aesthetic, by a series of reversals, displaces the rhythmic element from its source of power. By a final twist, song's being innocuous is necessary to speaking. Since song is mere decoration or decorum, spoken voice has less reason to expunge than to embrace it. Condillac: "The French recitative would lose in regard to us, were it rendered more simple, because it would have fewer beauties, without any appearance of nature."[26] Nature has been thoroughly tamed.

Singing the "words, vowels and phonemes" belongs to an art, as Condillac entitles Chapter VII, "Which is the most perfect prosody." Raising an aesthetic of spoken voice in the name of song is a later, perhaps the last, phase in the replacement which I have detailed of vocalic rhythm with phonemic interval. A look at its history reveals the tremendous odds that semantic cadence had to overcome in gaining supremacy over natural, proprioceptive resonance. Classical prosody with its close links to the musicality of song was able to inscribe rules of correct declamation. Having the script or score available enabled ancient performances to keep physically distinct the two modes, speaking in action and speaking in words. Separate performers pantomimed action and recited the speech. The distinction made it easy to isolate the rhythmic from the phonemic and to keep quantity from contaminating quality: "When gestures were once reduced to an art, and determined by notes, it was found an easy matter to subject them to the movement and measure of declamation." (II.I.IV.32)[27] By dramatically polarizing the desired and the undesired, ancient prosody could accomodate rhythmic extremes which would overwhelm present-day spoken voice. The advantage was lost in the distance from origin. The art declined with the influx of barbarian tongues. Nonetheless, the modern aesthetic of control permits us to utilize a substitute, namely:

> At the time of performing, we keep ourselves as calm as we can, without assisting the musician to draw us out of that situation; so that the sensations we feel, arise entirely from the impression of the sound upon our ear. (II.I.V.48)[28]

A mental indifference, the mind itself, now serves to insulate one from the enfeebling effects of unreasonable vocalic rhythm. Though loss of effect (for example, recovery of a basal somatic level of awareness) is inevitable, "this defect of our recitation is compensated by the advantage it has of appearing more natural to us." (II.I.VI.59)[29] The aesthetic of nature is in fact an aesthetic of the nonnatural, the artificial, the desirable. What is desirable is not sensation or its passional appropriation but rather the passionless, calming voice of phonemic authority. Why?

> It gives an air of truth to its expression, from whence it follows, that though it makes a much weaker impression on the senses than music, yet it acts with greater force on the imagination.[30]

In the end, Condillac's aesthetic, by which the wolves of the song are kept at bay, reduces to a theory of truth. That theory, of the air and not the ground, maintains its inflated value by adjuring contact with that which might puncture it, the syncopation of the song's voice.

Phonemic cadence, the interval, breaks the continuous control needed to sustain cognitive authority. An aesthetic replaces acoustic discontinuity. Such brokenness profoundly disturbs the becalmed mind. It calls forth memory of the discontinuity of signification. Henceforth, the aesthetic dictates rules of punctuation. Signs have a natural periodicity. A partial thought goes in the phrase or clause, indicated by the comma pause. A whole thought is a whole sentence. The period performs the stop, allowing in the rhythm of cogitation room for the subsequent thought. Condillac thus imports a foreign influence, punctuation, into the aesthetic. Never mind that the spoken word itself is not punctual and does not obey the rules of punctuation. The atmosphere of truth which perfect prosody breathes is supplied by the grammarians and syntacticians. The perfection which his aesthetic dictates has less to do with audibility and acoustics than with graphics and typography. He says:

> In a language, whose prosody is perfect, the succession of sounds should be subordinate to the fall of each period, so that the cadences shall be more or less abrupt, and the ear shall not find a final pause, till the mind be entirely satisfied. (II.I.VII.62)[31]

The art of perfection concerns the artificial, the mentally gratifying, the grammatically sound. Desire supports the aesthetic. Desire ensures that the ways we have of singing the world are intellectual. The song that never never stops plays on. With ears stoppered by phonemic domination, we never hear.

CHAPTER 8

How the deaf come
to speak

I am struck by the resilence of speech habits. Only an abrupt break in the automatism permits the voice of voice to sound. A focus on a totalizing and totalitarian phonemic control over voice, as I am attempting, does not annul the power to speak. Yet the momentary recognition of whose voice is lacking provides hope—if hope is a method. The awe of the dark woods takes speech away like the breath—only for a moment. Both nature and second nature return after the exclamation of voice dies in awareness. I do not find a regret in this fact since an echo of exclamatory awareness persists and may irrevocably transfigure speech. My search for a voice with its own intrinsic authorization, a voice of authenticity, begins with speech tinged with voice. Phonemic domination respects no inner authority but the rule of convention. Still, the sign does not extinguish an inborn response to the world. The incomparable value of voice's voice to expose the contradictory human condition is never fully replaced by aesthetic or moral value—value measured by the conformity of vocalic contour to a rule. The beauty of rightness of voice partially obscures its power to penetrate self-deception, reveal internal misalignment, harmonize imbalances, and uncover the consciousness of our humanity. The totalitarian claim is further advanced by an argument such as Wittgenstein's against a "private language." The claim asserts that the violent overthrow of the phoneme—voice returned to itself and the contradictions that it makes vocal—is a meaningless impossibility. The result would be only babble, random sounds (noise), or wild or insane cries. The argument makes a familiar reversal: liberated voice is made equivalent to a mute inner speech, a primitivism like Humboldt's *innere Sprachform* or an accomplished syntax like Husserl's mutism.[1] Deafness to voice's voice is the flip side of the originary metaphor. Recall there that one imagines an unknown x which added to voice produces the sign, phonemic contrast, and the "form of life" that ensures vocalic subservience. Solving for x then demonstrates that voice, in and of itself, is the bare physical substratum, the vocal apparatus, stupid and uninformed until empowered by the additive's intelligence. But various solutions for x—the cry, gesture, dance, song, and metaphor: the so-called precursors of speaking—met with no success. In each case, the unknown variable turned out to be speech in a bad disguise, a protospeaking intact with the signifier-signified relation, the replacement of need and desire by meaning-making volition, the effacement of vocalic prehistory, and the investment of a totalitarian political power to protect the privileged status of speech. In all cases, the resonant, vibratory, kinaesthetic, and proprioceptive qualities inhering in voice were kept concealed. Likewise the profoundly disturbing quality to reveal the condition of primordial war.

Where is the native authority of voice, apparent in babble, laughter, coughing, ecstatic exclamation, and crazed outcry, subverted? In the appeal of the metaphor of origin itself and its power to deafen ourselves to the condition our own suffering. For the raw, infantile, savage, brute, and contradictory desires of "prehistorical epochs," which are dispersive, divisive, and disparate, the self-calming desire keeps the conversation going among people. We need no longer hear the voice which voices our contradictory nature but listen to the one which speaks as we would imagine ourselves to be. Intellectualization of desire fanatically redefines action in terms of the sign. Imagination obscures the conditions impelling people toward a human consciousness. *That* desire, the desire to speak, becomes the *only* desire. Regarding the fundamental replacement, Wittgenstein, in the course of the argument that I just mentioned, gives insight by his terse observation:

> After all, one can only say something if one has learned to talk. Therefore in order to *want* to say something one must also have mastered a language; and yet it is clear that one can want to speak without speaking.[2]

The origin lies in one's initiation into speech. Voice plus speech equals speech; or what amounts to the same thing, voice equals zero. Speech is the originating matrix of desire, passion, and thought because it is self-originating. It even provides its own onto-genetical account: in the beginning was the word and the word was taught. Thus the origin replaces the transformatory war of human contradiction with its own phonemic and logical inconsistencies.

Initiation of the future citizen into phonemic rule is mimetic. One must want to speak, to replace the voice babbling with the spoken voice. "The substratum of this experience," Wittgenstein tells us, "is the mastery of a technique."[3] The desire to make voice spoken is fired by an impressive technology which displaces the infantile pleasure of sound production in both its acoustic and kinaesthetic aspects. Wanting to partake of the conversation requires surrendering the native resourcefulness of voice which is to explore the body and the body's external environment. Since one imitates only those who already made the sacrifice, independent evolution of voice is foreclosed. Deferred attention, referential priority, and articulatory control form the complex technology of the sign, specifying certain desires and erasing others. Saying that "the most difficult task facing the infant beginning to speak (as opposed to babbling) is *perceptual and imitative*, rather than articulatory," however, deemphasizes the newly instituted order of volition, the volition of the sign.[4] That regime supplies a critical force. It juxtaposes and correlates kinaesthetic impressions (of the vocal tract) and auditory impressions (of the ears). The pairing normally permits the replacement of babble with articulated sound.[5] The pleasure of unconstrained sound production gives way to the desire to signify. Jakobson takes significatory desire ("desire for communication") into account when he observes:

> There is a mnemonic connection not only of the kinetic and superimposed acoustic components, but also, and more important, with that

component of the speech sound concerned with content—*i.e.*, the sign-functioning element—to which the first two components are subordinated.[6]

He does not say that subordination is absolute, that the technology of desire absolutely supplants the free-style study of human volition, and that pragmatics of signification take the place of the ontology of innocence.

The crystallization of desire (for spoken voice) and the ability to attain its object (speech) are marked, like most initiations, by a discrete passage. The phoneme's authority displaces vocalic freeplay with surprising completeness. Jakobson says:

> The selection of sounds in the transition from babbling to language can be accounted for solely by this transition itself. *i.e.*, by the newly acquired function of the sound as a speech sound, or, more accurately, by the phonemic value which it comes to have.[7]

The displacement of babble by spoken articulation, moreover, has a surprising universality. Jakobson claims that regardless of mother tongue, prior history of sound production, or age, initiation involves only two consonantal units and one vowel unit. The infant technology is not immediately productive. The *coup de parole* is followed by the period of "phonemic poverty of the first linguistic stages," noted above. Not so apparent is the fact that the perceptiveness of voice is likewise impoverished. Jakobson: "The original self-sufficiency of the many disunited, individual perceptions is replaced by a conceptual distribution of articulated sounds, parallel to that of colors."[8] The very fact that voicing is perceptive—that sound production in itself with no external reference to the sign yields data revealing oneself and the world—is thereby erased. Self-resonance which senses the weight of things present by the particular acoustical vibration that it assays is forgotten. The membrane of perceptive audibility or audible perceptiveness which discriminates vibratory energies and allows response to their solicitations atropies. Its clairvoyant and omni-temporal properties are restricted. Thereafter, perception is regularized, categorized, and made mental. It is made to do the repressive work of citizenry with its desire for the spoken word. Jakobson observes: "As the child develops, the social factor becomes daily more important, while babbling is restricted to the leisure of solitary play and of waking and of going to sleep, and is later relegated to dreams."[9] Thus, vocalic

perceptiveness becomes a dream: once upon a time in a far off land . . .
Its relation to the consciousness of becoming human joins us only on
the rare occasion when a "certain" note is struck. No importance is
attached to the sound and the total response that it evokes because
sounds

> are subjected by the child to a selection by which they become speech
> sounds only insofar as they are related to language in the strict sense of
> the word, *i.e.*, to the "arbitrary linguistic signs," according to the
> Saussurean concept.[10]

But what of the deaf child? How do the deaf come to speak?
Concerning the correlation between kinaesthetic and acoustic impressions essential to phonemic valuation, they undoubtedly lack the
second. Nor can they experience the pleasure of vocalic perceptiveness, the prime force behind the phenomenon of babbling. Though
they begin babbling like a normal child, the babble gradually fades.
The deaf infant who cannot align its sounds responsively to its organic
milieu and the supporting environment cannot explore audible
sensitivity. But the disability is also a prophylactic. The same defect
renders the infant immune to the seizure of vocalic power by
phonemic authority. So Jakobson seems to argue

> that for normal development the acoustic impression of one's own
> sound productions is all-important, and that the child reacts to just this
> perceptual impression when he attempts to imitate his own sound
> productions in the process known as autoecholalia.[11]

Together, the silencing of babble and the articulating of phonemic
sound yield mutism, the solipsism of inaudibility. Whence the
customary link between defects of the ear and mouth: the deaf-mute.
 But does the impairment spare one from phonemic authoritarianism? That depends on whether the "acoustic impression of one's
own sound productions" is irreplaceable except by spoken voice. The
origin of the desire to speak, of the sign, of mastery in the technology
of speech, is the origin of replacements. This is the one-dimensional
aspect of players in *A Mid-summer Night's Dream*. One can stand in for
another. Articulated desire stands in for the self-contradictory will,
need for plentitude, absence for presence, artifice for nature, distance
and defeat for triumphant self-superimposition. By contrast, a lack of
substitutivity points to a recalcitrance in the will regarding initiation

into the sign. The defect of volition lies in the superiority, alleged by Jakobson, of hearing one's own voice. If the desire to have voice spoken is the supreme origin, an organic lack (such as Helen Keller's) would lead one to use other functionings to the same end. That desire already institutes phonemic authority, anterior to the power to execute that covenant, Saussure's *parole*. Desire inseminates with the sign without discriminating among the sensorium, the mind, and the passions. The deaf come to speak, like ourselves, by giving voice over to the sign. Only they do so in a world muter than our own.

The inference is most useful in revealing the conditions under which voice's voice sounds. Only we need to return to the primitive and phonemically deprived setting in order to make the correct deductions. Condillac supplies the material. Discussing the case of a ten-year-old "who lived among bears and who was found in 1694 in the forests that separate Lithuania from Russia," he reports:

> He gave no sign of reason, walked on his hands and feet, had no language, and uttered sounds that in no way resembled human sounds. It was a long time before he could utter a few words and even then he did it in quite a primitive way. (*A Treatise on the Sensations* IV.7)[12]

Having "no sign of reason" nor reason of signs, the Lithuanian child possesses a consciousness which while phonemically barren could "take care of his survival." The child lacks acoustical distinctions which, as Jakobson says, "must be capable of becoming impressed on the memory, and of being recognized and reproduced at will."[13] The distinctions themselves are only an imnportant accompaniment to spoken voice. They serve to activate cognition's power of retention which is then extended over larynx and respiration ("pneumo-laryngeal-buccal") for the purpose of articulation. Hobbes's imagination is the immediate agent of authority. Condillac confirms the fact that retention erases all data not retained: "As soon as he could speak, he was interrogated concerning his original state; but he remembered no more of that than we remember of what happened to us in the crib."[14] Condillac correctly sees that acoustics is no more essential to the spoken voice than is intonation, accent, and modulation. We can dispense with sound (or any specific sense) altogether since speech is the sign signifying the signifier. The audibility of voice when spoken is happenstance. Acoustics is a dispensible branch of the science of meaning.

Studies in the pathology of sound production, strangely, bear out the conclusion. The phenomenon of sound-deafness (complete or partial), so-called sensory aphasia, occurs when a person cannot grasp phonemic particles of his or her language. The traveler who struggles with foreign speech, the child, the senile, the brain-injured, and the Lithuanian boy, all suffer from it. Why sounds cannot be heard has nothing to do with the ear, but with "an intellectual deficiency relating specifically to language."[15] Regardless of whether the ear hears, a native Chinese speaker will not discern an *l* from an *r* in English. Jakobson concurs when he notes that the phenomenon "does not have its roots directly in the concrete acoustic, but rather in the conceptual, 'semiotic' sphere."[16] Only a matter of degree separates the victim of sound-deafness from the deaf person—as substantiated by its frequent correlate, sound-dumbness. So long as the cognitive element remains intact, a deaf person has the capacity for spoken voice.

What assault of cognition permits sound-discrimination, identification of word-signs, and comprehension of the voice as spoken to occur? With the Lithuanian boy, the uninitiated and phonemically inadept cognitive selectivity is not a given. He suffers, in Jakobson's words, from complete sound-deafness. The pathology stems from his use of animal voice, the ursine mother tongue. He is a foreign speaker in his homeland. His lack in the mental sphere is, however, a fullness which we, the initiated and adept, on occasion know. Of the striking truth of this knowledge, Condillac informs us:

> Sometimes our consciousness, that is to say, the awareness of what is happening within us, is distributed over such a large number of perceptions that act on us with roughly equal force, and is so weak, that it retains no memory whatever of what we have experienced.[17]

The fullness of consciousness means the absence of retentiveness. In undifferentiated awareness, the economy of poverty gains no foothold. The inseminatory advances of the imagination, spurred by eroticism and the desire for immortality, are naturally rebuffed. No trace is left because that remainder would make no difference to a consciousness replete with experience. The addition of the trace would be simply one more thing added to "a large number of perceptions" without affecting the total. The act of addition itself cannot occur since no percept decays, is made to be past, used up, and rigidified. The density of attentiveness, presence without distance, requires resourcefulness continually to integrate perceptual contents. No technology of fullness exists. Technology is invented only when plenty is lost. With the banishment of poverty and need, the work of self-will and its habit of distinguishing "mine" from "not mine" has no force. To the passion of retention, the condition is one of "lethargy":

> Then we are scarcely aware of our existence: days go by in a moment without our marking the difference; and we experience the very same perception thousands of times without noticing that we have already had it.[18]

To mark the difference retentively is the purpose of the new technology of the idea. To multiply the number of ideas is the means of keeping the awareness busy at the work of differentiating retentive marks, that is, at work rather than in "lethargy."

> The greater the supply of his ideas, the more reason we have to believe that one will find some occasion to awaken and to capture his attention in a particular way and to draw him out of this trance-like state.[19]

And what better way to spread fear and proscribe its economy than to use the speech of morbidity to describe the condition? The "deadened faculties" and life resembling "sleep disturbed only by dreams," no further element of disinformation is needed to root out cognitively undifferentiated awareness. In Hobbes too, we discover the same ploy used against the forbidden act of awareness. "Such are commonly the thoughts of men," he warns,

> that are not only without company, but also without care of anything; though even then their thoughts are as busy as at other times, but without harmony; as the sound which a lute out of tune would yield to any man, or in tune to one that could not play. And yet in this wild ranging of the mind . . . (*Leviathan* III)[20]

The technology to which Condillac alludes is that of deferred or derived attention. Attention is derived (and not pretechnological) when, as William James says, "it owes its interest to association with some other immediately interesting thing."[21] Primarily, attention is rendered derivative by the retentive power invested in "that most noble and profitable invention," speech. The rendering is, as Condillac acutely sees, a capture. Freedom to encompass a "large number of perceptions" is supplanted by fixation on the sign. The energizing effect of immediate perceptiveness gives over to the enervating complex of mental associations. The memory of retrieved signs replaces the living remembrance of wholeness. Concerning the Lithuanian boy, "it was thus natural," Condillac admits, "that he forgot his initial state."[22] The newly derived attention parcels plenary consciousness into manageable fragments. Awareness can summon up integrity. It disperses and isolates. The boy ceases to know the truth of a vital participation in reality. His primary acquisition from phonemic authority is the virtue of self-deceit. He can give no voice to how he came to be.

The deaf come to speak as the animal child who is completely sound-deaf does—as we all do. The technology of signification renders the attention deferential to the signified, breaking the integral of human consciousness and disposing thought, passion, and sensation to the service of conversation. To the derived attention, the preconceptual condition is the void, blank, fearsome, abyssmal, the waters of Lethe. To the primal state, cognitively speaking, belongs the fixity of animal voice, the bearish grunt. As soon as technology secures a beachhead, conversation is primed to begin. The case of the deaf-mute Ballard, as reported by William James, confirms the initial replacement which Condillac describes:

> I could convey my thoughts and feelings to my parents and brothers by natural signs or pantomime, and I could understand what they said to me by the same medium.[23]

From the forests of Lithuania to the cognition and passion indicative of civil conversation, the movement proceeds by means of the gesture. It can proceed, however, only because desire has already transformed itself, and the new economy, of poverty, of technology, of derivation, extracts the attention from its natural habitat. Once drawn from the organic milieu, the ever-present, "lethargic" body awareness, attention becomes discreet, circumspect, and dubious. It entertains and is entertained by the sign. It grows reflective. Ballard:

> It was during those delightful rides, some two or three years before my initiation into the rudiments of written language, that I began to ask myself the question: *How came the world into being?*[24]

The attention, grown pensive, has forgotten its primal state. Furthermore, to claim that Ballard could think without speaking (as James does) is to obscure the technological progress. *That* advance is already measured by his "speaking by action." A further string of questions which Wittgenstein raises compounds the obscurity:

> Are you sure—one would like to ask—that this is the correct translation
> of your wordless thought into words? And why does this question—
> which otherwise seems not to exist—raise its head here? Do I want to
> say that the writer's memory deceives him?—I don't even know if I
> should say *that*.[25]

To search for the cognitive precursor of speech: isn't this to search for
origin? Speech lives in an original lack, arising full-blown from the
sea-foam, ignorant of its pedigree. Ballard's gesticulations are already
speech, missing only the contingent factor of audibility. Whether the
words correctly translate them is the same problem as whether
"How'd ya do?" correctly renders "Comment ça va?" No reason exists
to suppose Ballard's memory of gesture is inherently faulty, for that
memory has already been technologically updated with the sign. It is
the memory that springs up to gratify the desire to speak. It may be "a
queer memory phenomenon," as Wittgenstein feels, but not the
intrinsically flawed operation of trying to remember events of
timeless, desireless, unsignifying consciousness.

The interchangeability of one technique of derived attention for
another shows that to bring the deaf to speaking presents no
insurrmountable (i.e., nontechnological) problem. The basic technology of the sign is multiplicity and mutation: how to repeat itself
endlessly, without gaps, to produce a universal algebra. Only then will
the abyssal lethargy of undispersed consciousness be eternally
avoided. Condillac recognizes in retentiveness the auto-genesis of
speech and the look-alike character of one stage and the next. As the
first speakers grew more

> familiar with those signs, the more they were in a capacity of reviving
> them at pleasure . . . . At first both of them acquired the habit of
> discerning by those signs the sensations which each other felt at that
> moment, and afterwards they made use of them in order to let each
> other know their past sensations. (II.I.I.3)[26]

The desire for conversation creates the presence of the past. In this
creation arises the gratification of desire. Not the immediate object
(speaking) but the derived one (remembering past signification)
brings the relief of temporary satiety. Like the attention, desire too is
deferred, put off, taught to be gratified with the secondary object.
Derived desire is deprived desire. Desire is made to live with its own

unsatisfiability and thus sustain its need to converse with the past in the nearness of the present. Communion with the past thereby relieves all desire of the means of verifying itself as desiring. When the object of volition is no longer at hand, one has no measure by which to assay its value. Its absence absolves one of the task of recognizing whether the want corresponds to the desired and the desired to oneself—whether desire is marked by truth or deceit. The volition of absence thus simplifies the requirement for translating gesture into voiced speech. Translation, replacement, or exchange is mere juxtaposition of similar signs for one and the same absented desire. It may be accomplished by rote. As Condillac says of the primal speakers:

> They articulated new sounds, and by repeating them several times, and accompanying them with some gesture which pointed out such objects as they wanted to be taken notice of, they accustomed themselves to give names to things. (II.I.I.6)[27]

Technology effects translation of speaking by action into speaking by words because it is spawned by the desire to translate—which is, to give speech to deaf ears.

The stage is now set for the development of sign systems by which the deaf are actually brought to speaking. "Sign language" is invented. The first entrepreneur perhaps is one John Bulwer whose *Chirologia* (1644) deals with the "naturell language of the Hand, as it had the happiness to escape the curse at the Confusion of Babel." Bulwer at once argues in favor of the interchangeability of sense impressions and the cognitive supremacy of the machinery of replacements. He writes:

> We have discovered sufficient ground to raise a new Art upon, directing how to convey intelligible and articulate sound another way to the braine than by the ear or eye; showing that a man may heare as well as speake with his mouth.[28]

His is a political art, another step toward actualizing the supreme power of the phoneme which Hobbes envisages. The radical equality of the senses, vital motion, and organic experience lead to the inclusion of all people—even the deaf—under the sovereignty of speech. The abolition of differences in sensory capacity, quality of desire, and attainment to human consciousness is complete. When the deaf speak, nature suffers a final defeat. When the deaf speak in signs, the soundless sound of the voice reveals its ultimate dispensability.

In Diderot, a century later, we find the penultimate solution. Interchangeability of parts, the yardstick of technology, is finally completed. His *Letter on the Deaf and Dumb for the Use of Those Who Hear and Speak* (1751) reframes Condillac's material on gesture for the special case of the deaf. Diderot offers a series of eccentric experiments to illustrate the intertranslation of gesture and speech (viewing a painting as a pantomime, listening to a theatre piece with the ears stoppered). As to translation per se, he shows surprising conservatism. We have hopes of giving the deaf speech only when we abandon hope of salvaging their actual experience. Conversation makes vocalic only the "analysis," its translated signification:

> The complete and instantaneous perception of this state is one thing; the detailed and continuous effort of attention we make to analyze it, state it, and explain it to others, another.[29]

The deaf, like ourselves, must adhere to the dictates of derived attentiveness. Full, immediate, uncognitive awareness cannot be replaced by the sign since its integrity leaves no window of opportunity for distance, derivativeness, deference. "Our mind is a moving scene," Diderot writes,

> which we are perpetually copying. We spend a great deal of time in rendering it faithfully; but the original exists as a complete whole, for the mind does not proceed step by step, like expression.[30]

Like ourselves, the deaf must learn of their sin. They too have fallen from integrity to fragmentation and absence, never to return. They too must recognize the disease of undifferentiated consciousness and combat it with the desire for conversation. Then the palliative will take effect:

> In the growth of language, decomposition was a necessity; but to *see* an object, to *admire* it, to *experience* an agreeable sensation, and to *desire* to *possess* it, is but an instantaneous emotion, rendered in Greek and Latin by a single word.[31]

For the deaf, like ourselves, speech, vocalic or manual, is loss and at the same time compensation for the loss. They and we are redeemed in compensatory speech only through the political union of conversation.

CHAPTER 9

THE POEM

I am so used to finding you innocent. There's an odd sentence. But how does it happen that the most honest expressions become the most ridiculous? In truth, we've spoiled everything, even the language, even words. Apparently, there's a spot of oil in the middle of things which has stretched to far that it has reached even to the corners.
Diderot, Letter to Sophie Volland, August 18, 1759

Voicing exclamatory existence, the poem (like the laugh and the breath) stands outside of history, beyond origin, erased. This does not surprise me. The breath itself may be a poem. Listen to Ahab's: " 'Befooled, befooled!'—drawing in a long lean breath—'Aye, Parsee! I see thee again—aye, and thou goest before; and this, *this* then is the hearse that thou didst promise."[1] The breath announces what speech forgets. The sounds that the poem breathes resonate with recollection. Yet within history, the bizarre optics of the originary point places the poem, along with gesture, metaphor, and myth, among the early precursors of spoken voice. All function as voice not yet confident of reference. Yet the poem, unlike babble, persists within adult conversation. It thus is stubborn and childishly unphilosophical. The poem is antiphilosophic when madly lyrical or insanely self-revelatory. Nevertheless Condillac defensively claims that "a philosopher, disdaining to be fettered by the rules of poetry, was the first who ventured to write in prose." (II.I.VIII.67)[2] The claim reveals philosophic prejudices. It fails to conceal the cognitive operations which render the poem innocuous, merely imitative, and politely tolerated. An important question therein arises. Does the poem speak words and thereby betray allegiance to the same economy of desire as does thought? In spite of itself, the repressive tolerance of speech belies a suspicion of the poem as other, as the unsignifying, unimagining, unerotic voice of human self-recognition. Granting the dangerous attraction, let us pursue the question.

The point at which the poem originates is particularly opaque. It is ringed with contradiction. Condillac superficially penetrates the inner circle. He notices that the poem expresses less exactly but more vividly than prose, it is pleonastic but suffers brevity, it is more memorable but less permanent, it is more sterile but more evocative. As "the style of all languages was originally poetical," so speech emerges from the slime of inconsistency to ascend to true nobility of denotation.[3] Contradictoriness only gradually gives way to referential precision, and then, first "among the northern nations" due to their "cold and phlegmatic constitutions." Natural geography supplies the chill to the erotically inclined imagination. The passions with which it seduces kinaesthetic awareness must be dulled in order for the more intellectual progeny to take command. Replacing gesture with word and multiplying signifiers both are important in order to forestall a vertiginous lapse into the undifferentiating, underived awareness, proprioception. Eventually, movement, modulation, and rhythm—the kinetics of voice—are "abolished by degrees, the voice admitted of less variety of tone, the relish for figures and metaphors . . . insensibly diminished."[4] The series of replacements serves to remove the ambiguous sting of the poem that cuts through our ordinary preoccupations to the intense terror of the primordial question. Not knowing who we are nor why we exist, we raise voice in the poem in the hope of eliciting a response. As the babbling infant, we explore a way of addressing that unknown force which vocalically interrogates us with regard to purpose, identity, and substance. Such a poem, predating the autonomy of pleasure, has nothing to do with pleasure. Leaving one profoundly disturbed, shaken, and without refuge, it throws into question the very economy of desire which gives phonemic meaning its life. That poem reawakens the inner war, "of one against the other," whose pitched intensity alone creates awareness of our human being. The poem's voice, voice's voice, destroys the illusions by which shame and self-deception deaden thought, feeling, and sensate life.

With his stake in the originality of the sign, Condillac has every reason for making the poem civil. For him, the ancient poem, though voiced, sings "of religion, laws, and heroes, only to excite sentiments of love, admiration, and emulation in the minds of the people." (II.I.VIII.75)[5] These "psalms, canticles, odes, and songs" were instructive. They "were cultivated merely with a design to promote the knowledge of religion and laws, or to preserve the memory of great men, and of the services which they had done to society." (II.I.VIII.72)[6] The poem is thus an early device for consolidating the victory of the phoneme over unphonemic voice. Later it will be supplanted by writing, an invention necessitated because "the promulgation of the laws could not, without difficulty, reach the ears of every individual." (II.I.VIII.73)[7] It allows the conversation of the polis to continue, uninterrupted by the antipolitical revelations of the human condition. It shapes thought and feelings to politically accepted standards of cognitive imagination. Most importantly, the poem trains voice to express desires of the political mind. It thereby emasculates voice by taming it with homily, custom, and philosophy—which is to say, prosody. In this way, voice and the poem eventually grow eloquent. And eloquence, one of "common conversation," suffices as the new measure of the poem's sound. The tremulous resonance of ineloquent voice, the sound that calls us back from the comforting sleep of desire to the struggle for human consciousness, that voice is laid to rest.

Eloquence in spoken voice comes to replace the shattering self-recognition of the voice's voice. What eloquence lacks is an inheritance since it itself derives from a lack of melody. Condillac says:

> As the prosody of the primitive languages fell very little short of melody; so the style of those languages affecting to imitate the sensible images of the mode of speaking by action, adopted all sorts of figures and metaphors, and was become extremely picturesque. (II.I.VIII.66)[8]

Melody, the musical combination of tone and rhythm, begins with the chant (*meloidia*, chanting). Percussive and tonal qualities of the audible frequencies localize in the hearer's awareness aspects of an address which invite his or her kinaesthetic response. The response is adequate only if global. Where the response is disproportionately mental, sentimental, or sensory, the auditor is at a distance from the voiced vibration. The ontology of absence prevails over that of presence. The phonemic or musical interval ceases to announce the enigmatic nearness of self and world. Distance repeats itself by replicating the distance in metaphor. Yet because the distance from the real to the signified is incommensurate, metaphor is absurd and absurdly necessary. Condillac acknowledges metaphor's absolute necessity in the primitive conjunction that it supplies: "that at the origin of languages mankind were under a necessity of joining the mode of speaking by action to that of articulate sounds, and of conveying their thoughts by sensible images." (II.I.XIV.138)[9] We are thrown back to the enigmatic place of metaphor in the history of voice. The conjunction, which is metaphoric, replaces a disjunction, which is real, but can never completely efface it. Metaphor may at any time betray its maternal roots in nonmeaning because speech feels the necessity of a coupling which it cannot encompass. Metaphor, the joint of articulated voice and voiced gesticulation, necessarily repeats the mystery. The hinge on which speech and gesture hangs, which opens in one direction to the sign, opens in the other to the nonsign. In one way, metaphor joins voice to phonemic authority. In another, it ruptures the joining by retracing the conjunctive point where the measured and the unmeasurable are drawn ineluctably together.

Condillac continues his defense of the court poem. The most eloquent poem dumbly obeys the rules of vocal prosody. It de-stresses metaphor. Eloquence is a civil virtue. Correctness in speech replaces the quest to fuse two disparate realms with the primordial ampersand of metaphor. Before metaphor is condensed and cooled by climate— and "affecting to imitate the sensible images" becomes mere embellishment—it transmits a voiced impression of the body in action and acted upon. Unknown forces capable of transforming kinaesthesis to a fully human consciousness are conveyed through the acoustic contour of voiced metaphor. Metaphor as such still contains the heat of attention. To that heat corresponds the pitch of inner warfare in which contradictory desires continually clash. Metaphor can dissolve what obscures the locale of battle, the body's awareness. The sudden shock of metaphoric resonance throws open a new relation to desire and need. The contingency of compulsion appears alongside of the phonemic authority which necessitates them to us. "The objects designed for relieving our wants," Condillac says, "may sometimes escape our attention; but it is very difficult for us not to observe those which are apt to produce sensations of fear and pain."[10] (II.I.IX.81) The moment of shock, during which replacement momentarily ceases and contradiction is heaped upon noncontradiction, is the decisive moment. Our choice is between which authority to place voice under: the phoneme or voice's own.

What about the phonic material of the poem? It is apparently phonemic. Fear and pain, the invisible hands governing the economy of desire, give their pinched shape to the desire for conversation. Their violent seizure of authority is metaphorically incorporated in the first denotations of objects. Condillac conjectures about the early inventors of reference: "it is very probably, for example, that they gave names to the wild beasts with which they were at war, before they had any particular names for fruits upon which they lived."[11] The logic of replacement shapes the economies of desire, passion, and need. Anguished desire violently displaces the struggle with one's weaknesses, domestic comfort displaces the fact of death, definition replaces ambiguity, mastery over technique replaces self-mastery. One war (attainment of desire) replaces another (relinquishing desire) under the name of peace. The acoustical design of metaphor, however, shatters the replacements. In it, an impression of the undenoted war survives, the way the echo of a bell survives the event that it announces or the way that the tone of a person's statement survives its logical point. Voiced anew, metaphor conveys the violence of its invention. In scattering the phoneme, casting momentarily aside the anguish of desire, voiced metaphor returns us to its original conjunctiveness. We encounter the choice to regain a completed human consciousness.

Approached from its cognitive side, metaphoric voice is the repetition of imitation or even of redundancy. It is born, the elder sibling of spoken voice, into the barren and impoverished state that voice has at its beginning. "The sterility of languages," Condillac says, "did not even permit them to express themselves otherwise: as these seldom afforded a proper term, they had no other way of explaining their meanings, than by repeating similar ideas." [12] (II.I.VIII.66) The equation of pleonasm and metaphor dates from the closure of the phonemic system. There, repetition, as Hume argues, must reduce to copying or repetitiousness or else it emerges with numerical identity. Accordingly, we are witness to a reversal of polarities, facsimile for authenticity. The metaphor lacks originality because it merely repeats what already is referenced. Yet the metaphor is at the origin because it satisfies the necessity to join the sign with the unsigned, unmeasurable, and real. Confining the voice of metaphor to the imitative narrows critical attention to matters of phonemic style; "every man thinks he perceives the copy in his own degree of sensibility." (II.I.VIII.78)[13] The other, or "native beauty," with which the metaphor has contact recedes in obscurity, being "so difficult to be found; too often it changes face, or at least it disguises itself in the dress peculiar to each country."[14] When we accept the indeterminate contact which metaphor formalizes, the polarities return to their initial value. Metaphor loses its innocuousness. No longer an embellishment of speech, it strips speech of reference. That to which metaphor binds speech resounds, throwing the meaning of spoken voice off center. The literal becomes the eccentric, the unstable, the hard to believe. The authoritative posture of the phoneme wavers as the play of human contradiction reappears. One is face-to-face with what the sign keeps hidden from itself: the incompleteness of humanity, its consciousness and desire. In its displacement of the sign, each metaphor repeats the original conjunction of reference with what is "so difficult to be found." Repetition is the insistence of nonclosure and ultimate self-righteousness of phonemic authority. The openness of metaphor consists of the archetypal *and*. The *and* is the irreplaceable in spoken voice. In that *and* lies the living memory of voiced reality.

The nonphonemic, nonimitative sound of metaphor is the voice of the poem. Such voice is the irreplaceability of replacement. Unspeechified voice which spoken voice represents as madness, babble, noise, or nonsense can be replaced by nothing. Nullity added to voice's voice yields spoken voice. Thus the poem is the acoustic dimension of proprioception. The poem takes the total kinaesthetic impression of the organism and audibly broadcasts it. The effect of voice's voice on the hearer is primarily kinaesthetic: to realign the other's body awareness to a state corresponding to that from which voice issues. The cough or laugh derives its penetrating power from this fact. Within the poem's voice, the mind plays the part of the nullity. It is present as a cipher. When it deciphers, interprets, or signifies meaning, mind acts as a saboteur, an agent of the state attempting to subvert the authority of human voice.

The action of the voiced poem is double. The first is to neutralize the cognitive imagination, the insemination of vital functioning, and the propagation of phonemic power. The second is to revivify body awareness to transform one's humanity. The double action of cognitive arrest and of proprioception is perceptively gleaned by Diderot. He notes:

Spoken voice is little more than a long series of sounds and of sensations primitively excited. The heart and the ears are engaged, but not the mind; it is by the successive effect of these sensations, their violence, and their totality that we understand and judge one another. (Salon de 1767)[15]

Violent vocalic rhythm replaces the erotic violence committed in the name of reason against the body. In that movement, the economic order which shame creates, whose essence of desire is self-deception, is overturned. The powerful negative passions of fear and anguish collapse. The dispersive power which keeps individuals and individual desires apart is weakened. One regains the capacity of self-recognition born of the fullness of kinaesthesia. Wanting what one hates and hating what one wants coexist but now with the awareness of coexistence. In that awareness, the desire for conversation is momentarily stilled.

The voice of the poem—regardless of its gentleness—necessarily assaults the listener with violence. The violation by phonemic domination calls forth a voiced response in kind. The interval between that voice and its comprehension is always filled with resistance. Where vital motion is held in check by the cognitive imagination, retention of significance becomes paramount. Nature, the unimpeded vital motion, the kinaesthetic sense, is de-selected by the attention. The body is tensed in its state of subjugation. The poem's voice brings the violent blow of liberation, the crack on the skull that suddenly brings one to his or her senses. "Whenever sensation is violent," Diderot observes, "or whenever the impression of an object is vivid and we are totally with the object, we sense, we do not think." (IX.356) The heightened resonance throws open the organism, rousing proprioception. The body displays itself to the double action of the poem's voice in two ways. It is enslaved to shame and the desire for self-deception. And it is the other, free and freely available to a relation with oneself. The body is revealed as a double, both the vehicle of the political economy of desire and the vessel of the self. The duality is revealed doubly in the impression that voice acoustically conveys and the impression of oneself. Diderot describes the doubling effect with great accuracy:

I play two roles, I am double; I am Le Couvreur, and I am myself. it is I, Le Couvreur, who trembles and suffers, and it is I who feels pleasure . . . . If I forget myself too much and for too long a time, the terror is too strong;

if I don't forget myself at all, if I remain myself, it is too weak: the correct
balance brings tears of delight. (XI.119-120)

In such an account, vocalic rhythm is not (as in Condillac) a
supplement to speaking by words made necessary by the demands of
imitation. There, rhythm catalyzes the translation of gesture into
word and disappears at the conclusion. It is a something that becomes
a nothing. By contrast, the voiced rebellion against phonemic authority requires in rhythm a violence which is substantially expressive. No
mere appendage to the sign, rhythm makes audible a specific state of
sensation. The acoustical form serves as a directive against the
repeated inauguration into speech. Its incitement is a prelude to
human consciousness. In the same way a high pitch shatters a glass,
vocalic rhythm transmits the disintegrating and reintegrating effects
of the poem. "What then is rhythm?" asks Diderot.

> It corresponds to the sensations [the poet] has and wants to arouse, to
> the phenomena whose properties he seeks to convey, to the passions
> which try him, to the animal cry they would elicit, to the nature,
> character, and movement of the actions he wishes to express . . . . It is
> the very image of the soul which is rendered by the inflexions of the
> voice, the successive nuances, the transitions, and the tones that are
> hurried, slowed, stifled, and tempered in a hundred different ways.
> (XI.268)

Rhythm carries the pulse of kinaesthesis from voice to ear. That pulse,
transmitted in terms of "a certain distribution of syllables, long or
short, hard or soft, muted or sharp, light or heavy, slow or quick,
plaintive or gay," indicates a circulation of vital motion. The auditor's
response, a particular expansion or contraction of sensation, recalls
proprioception to its central task: providing the consciousness of one's
humanity.

The organ of hearing is not the ear which remains under the
influence of the sign. Least of all, the ear that phonemically discriminates and comprehends. That ear makes the effects of music "the
subject of conversation," a further technology of political domination.
Hearing requires a renewal of voice prior to the designs of conversation, a listening to a basal somatic sensitivity. Hearing returns us to
the origin of origins, the experience of the infant. To displace the
replacements in voice incurs great danger. One abdicates the control
inherent in phonemic authority. Diderot reminds us of the perils of
confronting the voiced unknown. "In music," he says,

> the pleasure of sensation depends on a particular disposition not merely of the ear but of the whole nervous system . . . . There are . . . bodies which I would call harmonious, men whose every fiber vibrates with such quickness and force that in their experience of the violent movements of harmony, they sense the possibility of yet more violent movements, and get the idea of a kind of music which would kill them with pleasure. Then their existence appears to hang from a single taut thread which too strong a vibration could break. (I.408)

The voice that slays is the grotesque of the voice that slays self-delusion. It is violence not as means but as an end in itself; the double action halved. It is resonance directed by the dark vocalic intelligence, the Pied Piper who kills the rats and the children of Hamlin. That doomsaying also belongs to uncivil voice once desire no longer wears the dress of shame. The political security of the phoneme, like the metaphor of origin, is displaced by the state of war. In its brutishness, the almost absolute value of another life is not a given. Our unresponsiveness to the poem is ultimately a moral posture.

Where its violence encompasses the double action, voice does not threaten a "harmonic body" but only the body politic with dissolution. Voice explores an opening to one's disharmonious nature, re-equilibrating it, and transforming self-will into a responsiveness to the real. The profound disruption to one's life and its phonemic history impedes one's acceptance of the voice of voice. The radical transformation needed to fuse fragmentary consciousness requires a heat of attention which borders on cataclysm, apocalypse, and termination of knowledge. Diderot, for one, wants to dampen the newly uncovered uncontrolability of voice. Responding to critics of the *Letter on the Deaf and the Dumb*, he feels compelled to modify his views:

> These musical pieces . . . flatter your ear only in the way that a rainbow pleases your eyes, with a sensation pure and simple . . . . They are far from having the perfection which you could ask of them and that they would have if the truth of imitation were joined to the charms of harmony. (I.407-408)

Voice's voice is no longer perfect in its freedom from the sign, and so, perfectly untrue. Violence to the "truth" is attenuated by a familiar lack in its voicification. Voice, according to Diderot's modification, must become less than itself, must embrace the inferior and true by imitation. Mimesis always operates by replacement. The voice must lose its "pure" perfection which flatters only the ear and gain that of measure, reason, silence, and the sign.

We are familiar with Diderot's plan for the amelioration of voice. He requires that passion, as in Condillac, stand in the place of organic perceptiveness. Since the former is already signifying and the latter not, metaphor must be used to conjoin affectivity with sensitivity. We meet in Diderot a version of the originary metaphor. "Study the accents of the passions," he tells us,

> each passion has its own, and they are so powerful that they penetrate me almost without the help of the word. It is the primitive language of nature. The signification of a beautiful verse is not within reach of everyone; but everyone is affected by a long sigh drawn sorrowfully from the bottom of the guts. (Correspondance V.102)[16]

The emotions use a system of signification more primitive, more natural, than that of spoken voice. Speaking by words, as Condillac shows, replaces speech in the same way that one sign is translated into another. Diderot, like the legendary student of Heraclitus, takes the argument beyond its logical limit. The passions stand in the place of the irreplaceable—the unsignifying and unmetaphoric vital motion— because they (like voice, spoken or otherwise) penetrate in us to the proprioceptive level. We bodily sense the effects of anger, pity, joy, and jealousy. But in his intent to invert the terms, Diderot reverses effect for cause. He argues primitively that the cause must already contain the effect or else the former (cause) could not accomplish the organic transformation signified by the latter (effect). That is to say, passion carries its insignia into the flesh of one's flesh, absolving it of its innocence of signifying. In a grand reversal, passion itself becomes metaphor. Passion does the work of metaphor by joining the sign of one's state with its reality. Whereas before, metaphor was the invention of necessity, now passion as metaphor predates even the creation of the metaphoric bonding of the sign to the nonsign. Invented metaphor belongs to art and is merely imitative. Natural metaphor, passion, is constitutive of the real and is the basis of all sign systems.

Contrast this view with what the poem discloses. Sensation is essentially unsignifying. When the poem voices the body's sensate condition, the danger of sounding mad, babbling, incomprehensive radicals is heightened. That is tantamount to voicing the incommunicable which shatters the basis of all conversation. Diderot tries to bolster his position in two ways. On the one hand, kinaesthesis fails to provide matter fit to voice poetically. "Human sensations are incommunicable," he tells us,

> because they are diverse . . . . Suppose that God suddenly gave each person a language exactly analogous to his sensations. There would be no understanding at all. From Pierre's idiom to John's, there would be no synonym except perhaps the words "to exist," "to be." (II.325)

On the other hand, copying the primitive language of passion yields a defective, second-best way of speaking. While metaphor makes real connections between elements of reality, speech inevitably and mysterious fails accurately to replace the unspoken. Here is a subtle transposition of Condillac:

> I want to tell you about the accents proper to each passion. But accent changes in so many ways. It is a topic so fugitive and delicate that I know no other which better allows us to sense the poverty of all languages which exist and which have existed. (VII.107)

The result, however, is the same as Condillac's. Inventing a pan-metaphorism and making nature itself metaphoremic eliminates the dangerous possibility of sedition only by throttling the poem's voice. While the poem now imitates nature's poem, it never makes up the lack created by abolition of sensation. Its voice remains inferior and posterior no matter how richly inflected it is. The poem's kinesis which sets in motion forces to transform vitality into human awareness is stilled. Diderot's apostrophe to this impoverishment belies a longing for another voice. That voice, we know, in opening us to our terrifying poverty, opens the possibility of living beyond it. "How is it," he asks,

> that in the imitative arts this cry of nature, which is proper to us, is so difficult to find? How is it that the poet who knows it astonishes and transports us? Could it be that he reveals to us the secret of our hearts? (VI.304)

The poem's voice, the acoustic reproduction of natural metaphor, recaptures the original force of voice. Nearer to passion, more vocalic energy exists. But that voice is lost. "More energy," Diderot observes, exists among barbarian peoples than among political ones . . . . Everywhere, decay of energy and poetry as the philosophical mind has progressed . . . . It is unbelieveable the sickness this polite monotone causes in poetry. The philosophical mind fosters a dry, sententious style. Abstract expressions which include a great number of phenomena multiply and take the place of figurative expressions. (XI.131)

Yet the nearer to original passion the poem's voice moves, the more obvious its defect appears. Originality—imitating nature's imitation—is deceit. The poem which initially set its mark on human truth inaugurates the lie. Deception, the projection of the original abolition of the body's unsignifying kinetic force, is the play of the poem's voice. That play would be unchecked save for the critical intelligence with which phonemic authority is endowed. The poem's reproductive capacity is at once loss and gain, defect and art, truth and untruth, energy and distortion of energy. Cognition is required to supply the needed discriminations. Diderot:

There is in poetry always a little falsehood. The philosophical mind instills in us its discernment, and illusion and effect take leave. The first savages who saw a painted image of the prow of a ship took it for a real, living being and grasped at it. (XI.136)

The inventor of the original absence inflecting the poem with passional tones also invents the salvation. The mind redeems absence by explaining how the poem's voice is mere copy, and saves us by forbidding that we strive after the only apparently real.

Diderot betrays an ambivalence toward the poem's voice. The unrestrained energy of the poem provokes the awakening of existential terror. If we respond with self-deceit, our fragmented state is further broken. Then the time is "when the gods, thirsting for human blood, are appeased only by its spilling." (VII.371) Only by sacrificing our hidden shame and its cause, the cognitive imagination, do we uncover the quality that transforms partiality to wholeness, deception to clarity, the inferior to the superior, and phonemic oppression to the liberation of the voice. Facing the high risk, Diderot dampens the uncontrolable kinetics of the poem. Inimitability is supplanted with the imitation. Now the poem copies primal metaphoremes, the passions, which display nature already limited to the terms of emotional signification. One is not entirely safe within earshot of the poem, for identification with feelings may draw one to obsession, phobias, maniaical responses, emotional extremes. One is, however, safer than if overwhelmed by the raw energies of existence. In what does the safety consist? In avoiding the recognition of value which appears only when one obeys the unpremediated, unfelt response to dissolution. That value arises from the midst of the poem miraculously on its own.

CHAPTER 10

PLATO AND THE POETS

And we would allow her advocates who are not poets but lovers of poetry to plead her cause in prose without meter, and show that she is not only delightful but beneficial to orderly government and all the life of man.

Plato, *Republic*

Plato's political antagonism with the poets is inherited, not acquired. For "there is from of old a quarrel between philosophy and poetry." (*Republic* X, 607b)[1] With respect to the poet, Plato says "that we should be justified in not admitting him into a well-ordered state." (605b) The polis is founded on the rule of philosophy. The signifier-signified relation governs all vocalic action, inner and outer, mundane and eternal, profane and sacred. As for Hobbes, the *dedoublement* of the poet's voice for Plato strikes terror in the sound administrative mind. Especially suspect is the tragedian who creates "a vicious constitution by fashioning phantoms far removed from reality, and by currying favor with the senseless element that cannot distinguish the greater from the less, but calls the same thing now one, now the other." (605c)

Thus the poet who calls us to recognize our prepolitical selves ought, morally and prudentially, to be kept beyond the city's walls.

Plato's cautionary measure with regard to the cognitive element that I am examining needs to be studied. Might the poet's voice, voice's voice, be after all included in the polis? The poem itself gives testimony to the wisdom of Plato's course. Oedipus, blinded and shattered in his ego-identity, uses that voice as he takes leave of Thebes:

> After bearing such a stain upon me, was I to look with steady eyes on this folk? No, verily: no, were there yet a way to choke the fount of hearing, I had not spared to make a fast prison of this wretched frame, that so I should have known nor sight nor sound; for 'tis sweet that our thought should dwell beyond the sphere of griefs.[2]

Having suffered the collapse of phonemic authority and the fury of human contradiction, Oedipus's voice no longer speaks the secret grief, the self-concealed discovery of defect, shame. He gives voice to that unity established through pain—himself. Knowing its effects on the polity, he wishes himself deaf as well as blind. Oedipus does not, however, aspire to muteness. Had he, a place might have been reserved for him in Plato's state. With his tongue gone, he could no longer have urged the mad search for human consciousness. Mute, he would have grown philosophical.

Plato, as is known, was a poet. Some say his embrace of philosophy has a hidden and poetic agenda. In any event, the philosopher's exaggerated name-calling toward the poet—"the yelping hound barking at her master and mighty in the idle babble of fools"—smacks of irony. (607b) Irony is a familiar device for a double message. It redounds throughout his version of the originary metaphor in *Cratylus*, which I now consider. In the account, success, referential precision, and truth in spoken voice all derive from knowledge of speech's arche. The philosopher whose instrument is signification (as the shuttle is the weaver's) must be aware of a "natural" correspondence between the vocalic sign and the mutely signified. An arbitrary acoustic determinant, the articulated sound ("the natural instrument"), results in the misframing of names ("as things ought to be spoken"). (*Cratylus* 387c) Fidelity in vibration coincides with correct denotation. The origin, as Hobbes, Condillac, and Diderot suggested in other ways, mysteriously bears the acoustical signature of truth. If only the ear were keener . . . Then one need not rely on metaphor to bridge the irreducible gulf between sign and presence. Then one could learn, as Adam from God, "how to name such creatures as He presented to his sight." (*Leviathan* IV)[3] The enigmatic work of divine phonemics is rendered for Plato not by the Hermetic priest but by the legislator. The lawmaker is the miracle worker. He is able "to put the true natural name of each thing into sounds and syllables, and to make and give all names with a view to the ideal name." (*Cratylus* 389d) He alone attends to the originary point without deflection, distance, or decomposition. Or rather, he is truly daemonic, combining continuity and the interval, need and plenty, eros and thanatos, madness and reason. We are prepared for the irony of Plato's answer when Hermogenes asks to be shown "what this is which you term the natural fitness of names": "I have none to show." (*Cratylus* 391a)

The joke is taken a step further when we consider Plato's "nature." The lack of exemplary evidence to offer Hermogenes replaces no lack in the name-sound as it imitates the thing. Unlike with Hobbes, Condillac, or Diderot, the lawmaker's copy introduces no element of absence by the act of naming because in fact such naming is not speaking. Whereas for the others "nature" already includes the interval of distance in the cry (Hobbes), the gesture (Condillac), or the passion (Diderot), the case is otherwise for Plato. The thing in its nature is a fullness which is forever inert. Nothing can be added or subtracted from it by its natural name. The sound which names the thing for Plato is both full and fully inert. Its acoustical contour is a copy which is not a copy. Suffering no deprivation of forcefulness, energy, or power, the sound expresses "the essence of each thing in letters and syllables." (423e) If you want, the sound is a sympathetic vibration of the resonant nature of something. It cannot, therefore, be repeated at will, if will involves the cognitive imagination articulating the organs of speech. Such a sound cannot belong to a system of signs which are phonically reproduced in spoken voice. The lawmaker himself does not speak the name-sound. It is spoken through him in the way that a cough or a laugh passes vocalically through a person. In that originary plentitude, the nonsignifying of names only increases the enigma of the voice of speaking.

The mysterious "imitation of the essence" attaches denotations not spoken at will. The lawmaker, like Adam, reiterates the archetypical creative act each time that the "natural" sound passes through his vocal apparatus. Phonology recapitulates ontology. Just as complex creatures are combinations of elements, so name-sounds combine the basic particles of articulation, the phonemes. "Ought we not, therefore," Plato asks, "to separate the letters, just as those who are beginning rhythm first distinguish the powers of elementary and then of compound sounds?" (424c) Divine phonemics yields the science of presences. It is the alchemy of primitive energies which in combination mimic the creation of the world. Within the human frame, however, it produces no system of representational signs, but things in themselves. For Plato, the lack of absence does not restrict the lawmaker's denotative reckonings. His superior audition—which "looks to the name which each thing by nature has, and is able to express the true forms of things in letters and syllables"—is, moreover, the *sine qua non* for successful political leadership. (*Cratylus* 390e) To reframe his omnipotent phonemic authority is to bend the speech of the state, to debase it, to inject the element of failure. The basis of the polis is not conversation (Hobbes) but acoustical divination.

Speech of presence, with its close connection to essence, form, and nature, repeats without loss or gain, the resonant integrity of the eternal object. It is, therefore, not ordinarily known. Absence, need, and desire customarily apply phonemic authority to voice, making it merely representative. Speech of distance, as Saussure indicates, simultaneously represents the speaker and the sign system. Plato's mode of voicifying requires annulment of both. "I" as Cartesian ego ceases to speak. I am spoken through by voice. We are surreptitiously returned to the primordial war. Cessation of accepted standards of personal identity is plainly seditious. Conversation, the art of keeping company, supposes the existence of distinct egos. The economy of desire based on poverty supposes separation and dispersal of individuals. Thought and passion likewise belong to persons in their cognitive isolation. Voicing in a way that "objects should be imitated in letters and syllables, and so find expression" means surrendering the confinement of the individual ego. (425d) It means restoring the existential center of our humanity around which revolves the covert war of contradictions. Before that, it means recovering the proprioceptive basis of consciousness together with the means of imitatively responding to things in their acoustical, vibratory natures. The requirement for the recollective movement is enormous. Small wonder that Plato announces with chagrin, "My first notions of original names are truly wild and ridiculous." (426b)

Does he retreat to a safer account? He rejects two. The first is the version of the originary metaphor chosen by Hobbes and the others. It explains names by "deriving them from some barbarous people." (425e) We end up with the equation, voice plus x equals speech. That account, we saw, introjects an irremedial lack in voice in order to yield the phoneme, signification, and the political order. Vibratory fidelity, coherence, and integrity, which directly affect the kinaesthetic state and state of consciousness, are replaced by a notion of representational truth. The representative that brooks no rivals and conceals the defect of its creation then erases the act of replacement and establishes history. To explain the superior and more highly intelligible result from the inferior, less informed antecedent, moreover, requires a disguised version of the former present at the beginning. Hobbes, Condillac, and Diderot all succumb to placing the sign before the sign. Plato refuses himself that course. That leaves the second, Adam's way of naming things, or—to return to the subject at hand—the tragic poets' whose word is that "the gods gave the first names, and therefore they are right." (425e) But the *deus ex machina* deplores of finding an originary fitness in the spoken word. Therefore, the acoustical sympathy between the phoneme and the thing itself supplies the required, though difficult, explanation.

I am looking for the path between two impossible avenues. Are the poets deprecated in the *Cratylus* the same who are guilty of practicing their mimetic arts in the *Republic*? Evidently not, since the *Republic* lot engages in treason while the *Cratylus*, plain bad sense. Treason falls short of the seditious behavior of the practitioner of divine phonemics. Nonetheless, Plato reserves some of his best invective for the treasonous gang. Though their crime implies acceptance of the phonemic yoke, their culpability lies in taking certain liberties with it. They are degenerates. They bring down the republic in the way in which lying undercuts the institution of truth-telling. Like Homer speaking about medical arts, they know nothing about the natural names of things or the derivative arts. The poet is a copyist of a facsimile. Failing to understand what essence a sign lacks with respect to the object, he replaces that absence with another based on the accidents of phonemic fashion, "rhythm, meter, and harmony." (*Republic* 601a) Rules of inflection, secondary qualities of spoken voice, replace cognitive signification—itself a replacement for the natural attunement of voice with the world in the *Cratylus* account. Loss of true phonic substance becomes irreversible. With that loss comes phonemic destruction and death. Such is the heinous crime of the poem.

But how exactly does the poet commit a crime? In the *Republic*,

Plato accuses the poet of supplanting the greater by the lesser, work by play, and reference by inflection. Mere replacement is no criminal act—unless phonemic authority is criminal. The poet's crime is to reach truth by deceitful means; his insolence is to encroach on the legislator's right to lie. (*Republic* 389) His threat to referential truth is to brandish the truth of human contradiction. Because his art operates directly on the cognitive imagination, his results challenge political conversation. Within the space of inversion, he cleaves passion and desire from the object. He then reattaches an arbitrary object, a new grief, pleasure, or delight. Havoc is played with the economy of desire. In the economy of scarcity, shame projects a stoicism to deal with the inevitable thwarting of desire. The secret of phonemic authority, of cognitive defect and violence, requires concealment of human suffering. For political unity is achieved on a strictly pragmatic basis. If citizens acknowledge that they suffer more than when they were "natural," the self-recognition would bring madness and insurrection. Necessarily, the manly virtues—temperance, calmness, unflinching self-restraint—displace the feminine ones—sympathy, passionate abandonment, and emotional expressiveness. Political values require, as Plato says, an "ability to remain calm and endure, in the belief that this is the conduct of a man, and what we were praising in the theatre that of a woman." (*Republic* 605e) The crime of the poet is his revaluation of the feminine. Not the rekindling of passion *per se*, but the disclosure of the passions of suffering constitutes political criminality. Emotion in and of itself can be restrained within the repressive limits of the state. Bring suffering into view, by contrast, and one rouses consciousness of the self who suffers. One sees the contingent causes of its immiseration. The revelation that desire and need, in the context of the republic, cause suffering creates conditions for the overthrow of violence with violence. Only asserting masculine, authoritarian values at the start precludes self-recognition. Speaking of the "effect of poetic imitation," Plato displays these values. He says:

> It waters and fosters these feelings when what we ought to do is to dry them up, and it establishes them as our rules when they ought to be ruled, to the end that we may be better and happier men instead of worse and more miserable. (606d)

The conclusion is obvious. Within the republic, no poets allowed.
    Voicing the self-evidence of human suffering absolutely ex-

cludes the poet from political society. Along with the lover, the fanatic, and the mystic, Plato might have preemptorily excluded him as mad. The unreason of the poet, which is exposed in the *Phaedrus*, identifies him as a rebel to phonemic authority, cognitive imagination, and shame-laden desire. One way or the other, both arguments bypass the primordial voice of the *Cratylus* whose imitation is of another order. I want to make room for the poet's reentry by the alternative route. Plato says little about the audible "imitation of essence." But he suggests that the "sympathetic vibration" which vocalically moves the poet gives time and place to what was only ideational. Rhythmic and tonal patterns of physical voice make data available to human (but not only human!) life which was available only to suprahuman creatures. Thus imitation partakes of creation. One may on other grounds suspect that the creational dimension of voice relates to Plato's hidden program for the poet. For instance, Diotima, in the *Symposium*, takes a surprising view "of poetry in the true sense of the word—that is to say, calling something into existence that was not there before." (*Symposium* 205b) The poet's voice therein substantiates in its sound what was hitherto a potential energy, a vibration without locale, an acoustical form without a content. The naming is a birthing. The function of the poet's voice is maieutic: to assist at the passage of the unknown, unfelt, and unsensed event, belonging to a higher domain, into the realm of human consciousness. That voice is, however, additive. Added to the vague, preconscious strands of reality, it allows novel unity to emerge. "To the many, one is added, and it becomes one."

Necessarily, the poet's voice, voice's voice, by-passes the retentive mechanism of cognition altogether. The dispersive, differential operation of thought is as unreceptive to the data which voice transmits as the eye is to audible sound. Voicing existence is directed, not to the Cartesian ego, but to the membrane capable of perceiving existence: the proprioceptive film upon which human consciousness is based. Existence, unlike the essence it imitates, vibrates with the frequencies of organic life. These vibratory energies leave their impression on the organ of internal sensitivity. The impression becomes a necessary element in the transformation of body awareness to fully human consciousness.

Not so with regard to essence. Whatever else Plato says about essence, its imperceivability is most striking. Nothing in sensitivity responds to its vibration. No matter which way we open to sensory experience, the essence, form, or nature of a thing lacks an impression. The lack—of direct contact with essence—is translated via the sign-system into absence, distance, derived attention, the unbridgeable interval between signs, between desire and its object, between individuals. Cognition concludes that the particular must be deduced from the assemblage of its sensory properties, the whole from the parts, the integer from the fractions. The inference is, however, from sign to sign, never to existence, the impingement of essence on organicity. Existence "is not a predicate" and so enters into no signifier-signified relation. Existence is never captured by a sign-system and forever offers proof to the limits of closure. It is a something which adds nothing to a sign, an anomalous fact, a datum recalcitrant to phonemic authority. Existence, as seen, can be phonemically approached only indirectly, through metaphor. If direct evidence is sought, the Cartesian ego is forced momentarily to an acknowledgement in the self-pronouncement of spoken voice. "I am," "I exist," is true, not by virtue of reference, but by the vocalic heralding of existence. In the moment of voicing, an organic response to the acoustic impression leads to an affirmation of one's particular humanity. One announces the arche-name—I. Choice of the sign is incidental to a consciousness opening to the audible resonance. The advent of one's existence, when assisted vocalically, does not come by way of phonemic contour or the politic semantics of desire. Descartes's discovery has more to do with the arousing of kinaesthesis than with a grammar of existence.

The awakening sense of existence springs from a certain nonreferential leap from the signified thing to its being. In perception, that leap corresponds to the activation of proprioception. A double movement is involved. First, the attention which defers to phonemic authority must be recouped. When not derivative, an attentiveness ceases to be at the service of deriving one sign from another. It becomes its own authorization. It is free to enter relations for which it has a natural affinity. Second, the attention must be allowed to circulate through the body, its habitat. In this fashion, it immediately joins with the vital motion. Through contact with sensation, the body's native perceptiveness is reanimated. A new "ancient" mode of recognizing objects through their existences is thereby engaged. The mode is dark and prelucid. Unlike the bright mode of vision which is laden with cognitive elements proprioception does not utilize definition, contour, interval, or distance. It senses presences. The interior circulation of the underived attention makes the body permeable to environmental energies. The internal sense of the body registers their existences.

Primordial voice of which the *Cratylus* speaks vocalizes proprio-ceptive data. The special qualities of voice's voice broadcast states of the body's milieu: breath, pulse, and the tempo of the circulating vital motion. These states echo the internal contractions and expansions of the body's awareness in the presence of a resonant energy. When the appropriating tendency of the economy of desire has been fully neutralized, they faithfully echo the impact of "the essence of a thing" on organic human life. More commonly, desire is only partially neutralized and disinterest, incomplete. Voice's voice then makes audible an interference pattern of proprioceptive data overlaid with the retentiveness of phonemic control. The degree to which the existential register of the essence is manifest depends on freedom from retention. Where the attention is taken up by the mission of the sign, absence reigns. Where it is released to the circulation of vital motion, the presence of presences is restored. The fact is that voice most frequently voices the lower ranges of existential perception. The deflecting force of phonemic authority is very strong. As a result, voice more often makes audible the impression of what occludes presence. The interference pattern echoes the integral of propriocep-tion plus the distraction of conversation. The addition which is a subtraction is the vocalic experience of human suffering.

The fate of the poets in the *Republic* must be reviewed in this regard. Plato's act of expulsion stems from their disclosure of suffering. He has two reasons, a lesser and a greater, corresponding to the double movement of the disclosure. The poets' audience, Plato deplores, responds in an expansive fashion, in "that the best element in our nature, since it never has been properly educated by reason or even habit, then relaxes its guard over the plaintive part." (*Republic* 606a) The poets' voice bears audible witness to the contradictory strivings of the economy of desire, the self-deception to create it, and the masculine repression needed to sustain it. By its interrogation, suffering opens one to the feminine virtues which guard the existential register of perception. The danger is that one grows satisfied by mere emotional expressiveness, catharsis, and the inflated life of feeling. Disclosure of suffering may rouse a love of the rhapsody. Homer again exemplifies this trait:

> He smote his breast and chided thus his heart,
> Endure, my heart, for worse hast thou endured.
> (*Odyssey* 20.17-18)[4]

Plato, however, berates "clapping one's hands to the stricken spot and wasting the time in wailing," without carefully distinguishing it from the reverse movement. (604d) Suffering reveals the hiddenness of concealment. It brings out the secret shame on which the reversals of phonemic authority turn. It thereby removes the obscuration to the proprioceptive membrane which contains all conscious insights. Suffering ultimately points to the suffering body, its repressed desire and perception, and through it, to the body sensitized, responsive, and whole.

Voice's voice sends essential energies, otherwise unavailable to perception, into existential orbit. The acoustical "imitation" of trans-human reality by proprioceptively endowed voice creates the poem of immediacy, presence, and noncognitive intelligence. Though cloaked in semantic trappings, its movement is essentially recollective: to restore one to integral awareness of humanity. Its operation is kinetic. By the breath, the pulse, and the circulation of vital motion, its acoustical content realigns the retentive relations between passion, desire, and thought. The new relations are informed by a reality superior to the politics of signification. Cognition, emotion, and sensory experience express the existing self and are transformed in novel and unpredictable ways. The poem's nullification of cognition is the cancelling of an unthoughtful functioning, not a total abolition. The indirect effect is to remake the intellect in the image of the total being. If the action is meant "to destroy the rational part," the poet is guilty of unreason. (Republic 605b) If destruction is necessary in order to remake the mind, the poem's voice supplies the means.

Ambiguity is the stuff of metaphor. Ambiguity infects the political role that Plato assigns the poet. We should be on guard for the workings of metaphor, its fertile way of binding the sign to the real and reversing the polarities. Recall the charges. The tragic poet is exiled for his effeminate voice. That voice, of the suffering of the human condition, weakens the moral (i.e., masculine) fibre of cogni-tion. Once enervated, the cognitive imagination must face its vio-lence, its self-deception, and the role which conversation plays in camoflaging its defect. The intense encounter, revolutionary in scope, of the mind with its secret life returns voice to its origin. That is Plato's version of the originary metaphor. Human suffering strips voice of speech and restores it to itself. Speech is a substitute for suffering human incompleteness and a replacement for the task of becoming complete. Voice minus suffering equals speech. Speech is a negative whose subtraction is a plus. Unphonemic voice reveals suffering and suffering reveals whence voice comes. Voice begins in the midst of suffering, when the expanse of existence will brook no repression. The dangerous fecundity of the tragic poet, for Plato, lies in his relation to the arche. He is of course a master at crafting the spoken word. Yet he experiences what reduces speech to nothingness, the immense anguish of human contradiction. The charge which Plato levels has to do with his special knowledge. This knowledge makes him a potent antidote to all that the republic represents: the state of representation. With the force of self-recognition, the voice that he wields calls the politics of the phoneme into question. As Oedipus told us, the truth of suffering discloses the movement of deception— which is, in its wildest form, the substitution of an imitation for the real thing.

One further twist remains in the intrigue against the poets. Tragedians ought to be exiled, Plato argues, since they practice knowledge which is seditious. But the argument trades on the reversals which the apologist to phonemic control deploys. When Plato says of the poet, "if he had genuine knowledge of the things he imitates he would far rather devote himself to real things than to the imitation of them," he by sleight of hand gives the poet's critique of the philosopher. (*Republic* 599b) Within the republic, the philosopher assents to substituting phonemic control for voice made naked by suffering. That voice alone is transformative. Operating on the raw material of body awareness, it incarnates the full potential of a human consciousness. The philosopher betrays its workings for the hegemony of the phoneme. When we look at the poet, what he does is to imitate in precisely the way outlined in the *Cratylus* account. His struggle lies in finding the way between phonemic control and its surrender. At the origin, where the two axes intersect, conditions for a novel kind of voicing appear. The retentiveness of cognition melts. A proprioceptively endowed vocal apparatus operates. Transhuman energies of essences, the eternal objects, are brought to the human vocal fold. The poet as a vessel of vital motion is vocally instrumented. The voice allows existents to stand forth from the background of mute self-deception. It discloses the human self along the trajectory of consciousness. That self-disclosure of noncognitive knowledge is patently one of "first names." Specifically, it is knowledge of the first of all first names, "I." It exhibits the creativity of reality, not, as the philosopher has it, of phantoms.

Such originary voicing of essential, transhuman energies is, to be precise, not the poet's. At its occasion, the structure of replacements which is his Cartesian ego is voided. He is the spectator who

participates in the phenomenon but has no special claims of owner-
ship. As recipient of the gift of naming, he is possessed by the process.
Hence he fails Plato's test of knowing the means of his mimetic art:
"the imitator will neither know nor opine rightly concerning the
beauty or the badness of his imitations." (*Republic* 602a) He is
cognitively ignorant with respect to his voice. Nonetheless, his
ignorance belongs to an order quite apart from the arrogance of
phonemic authority which is oblivious to the act of naming. Plato's
warning in this regard comes full circle and can only be aimed at
supporters of political conversation. He says:

> And yet any sort of ignorance of first or primitive names involves an
> ignorance of secondary words, for they can only be explained by the
> primary. Clearly then the professor of languages should be able to give a
> very lucid explanation of first names, or let him be assured he will only
> talk nonsense about the rest. (*Cratylus* 426a)

AFTERWORD

Under the reign of Hermes, sovereign power of exegesis, music, and theft, truth is photophobic. It hides from the light. In concealment, a trace of the hiding lawfully is left. To ferret the hiddenness out into the light is to bring the cycle again to its beginning. Though the task has a Sisyphusian rhythm, hermetic repetition is a different, more hopeful action. Through it, we are called with increasing intensity to the moment of escape when the truth vanishes. Here perhaps is the point at which philosophical study begins. The mysterious force that absents us as truthful witnesses demands that we exchange our place with it. Until we are able willingly to face the replacement, it proceeds willy-nilly. What eventually enables us is the revelation of difference, that we need not step aside in deference to the other because we are ourselves irreplaceable. That is a, or the, end-point of philosophical work. That it lies at a great distance from my present study, I only note—though not too distant to place it squarely on the board.

I make these remarks in order to air some dangerous thoughts. The danger of cleaving too closely to authenticity is meek pretention. I have sought the authentic ring of voice—the voice of myself—to lure it from hiding to invite the moment of self-recognition. That such moments have emerged I do not deny. The study records their appearance. But I proceed and have proceeded by means of words, signs, and graphic counterparts to articulated expression. And so I must. Does this not place me at the same tangled distance which, as I argue, obscures me from my own voice? If so, is the present study any less deceitful than the history of philosophy that it belabors? Temptation is to ally myself with the hidden trace that never fully leaves existence. In the poem, the position has some justice. The poem is made for voicing and suffers incomparably from subvocal recitation. Since I bring a philosophical study and not a poem, I resist this suggestion. Instead I accept the objection, adding only that it does not go far enough. The discrepancy between my logical claims for revealing true voice and my means of proceeding is real and irreparable. Concealment, therefore, is a mute partner to the written enterprise of discovery that I conduct. It is inescapably so. In defense of the project, I would say only that the deception is a greater one than the history that it opposes. It is greater because more is promised. The hiding is not thereby justified. Being necessary, it requires no justification. I mean only to indicate that the deeper concealments have correspondingly deeper recognitions. To elicit a phenomenon of depth requires greater risks. None is greater than the risk of hiding discovery behind mere words.

What is promised? The incomparable moment of recovering oneself in the midst of voice. The moment does not then terminate but echoes throughout the field of activity. It may sound even during reading. If the memory that resonates to the special overtone has grown more animated, the study assists one's responsiveness to opportunities along the way of return. By contrast, if one is reminded only of a certain order of signification, the hiddenness of voice has been strengthened. The greater risk lies there. One's capability to speak about the subject more effectively takes the place of recognition. The work of voice (to recall oneself to oneself) is more naturally replaced by the work of speech (to recall analysis, exposition, and commentary). I know of no antidote to the risk. Even to confront the jarring of intellect by unaccustomed thought guarantees no real result.

Another factor is also at work. It contains a hope of mine. To bring concealment under study is to render it more or less transparent. Transparency is not innocuousness. Attention to the law of hiding may make one more aware of the vanishing point but does not eliminate the hermetic action of truth. Transparent concealment gives, however, a way of understanding metaphor. In order to allow true voice to sound in me, I tell (in writing) a fable. It is a fable about the loss of one's voice, my voice. Other philosophers have told of the gain in speaking but speak in fable nonetheless. The action of the fable that I tell is displaced. The moral of the fable (Aesop's, for instance) always acts at a distance, unveiling itself unexpectedly in the midst of an experience. The person whom one hears saying, "Sour grapes," is oneself. I catch in myself the fabulous character of the fox. The action precipitates a self-recognition. Similarly with the fable of the voice.

Though constructed with signs, one encounters its action and its moral in the midst of giving voice to an aspect of oneself. At that moment, one is returned the person of voice, oneself, acoustically clear and present.

These remarks may throw some light on my relentless opposition of the cognitive to the kinaesthetically noncognitive or of articulation to resonantly free sound production. From the logical point of view, in any opposition lies hidden the mysterious point of reconcilation. There is the Hermetic fountain. Logically, if one seeks the conditions under which that point is disclosed, any opposition is of equal value. Either arm of a single opposition is equally suspect since the other must be concealed within it by obscuration. Where the polarities are treated only as signs, my favoritism toward kinaesthesis and unrestrained resonance is oddly uncritical. From the viewpoint of metaphor, however, other factors dictate choices favoring one pole over the other. In metaphor's transparent concealment, the sign is slightly displaced from its merely signifying function and so to speak dangles closer to the face of reality. (Parenthetically, the opposition metaphoric/literal is subject to logical and metaphoric considerations similar to any other.) The law of metaphor, as said, is action at a distance which, through fable, appears at the moment of self-recognition. Metaphoric choice may seem logically capricious, protean, arbitrary, biassed, and unjust. Rational morality certainly opposes it. Nonetheless, stressing a single polarity is at times metaphorically efficacious. The design of the present study is to approach the point at which the opposition of speech to organic resonance (and of cognition to proprioception) collapses. Because the second polarity is submerged in the first, I have found it metaphorically efficacious to stress the former. Other fabulists might do it differently. My motive for emphasizing the body's voice over cognition's is partially to redress the injuries of history and partially to acknowledge a precedence in the order of existence. The test of my choice ultimately is practical. Does the action of the study return oneself to the sounding in one's voice?

A final point. These remarks may help forestall the impression that cognition is inherently mischievous and given to deception. I do not recommend supplanting or remaking its function which is absolutely essential. If cognition did not exist, we would have to invent it. If we are hermetic creatures and the truth photophobic, some means of deferring the attention from our own existence is inescapable. To grow transparent to the function is not to cease to defer (as logic points out) but to seek a way of return to the concretely embodied moment. One (but not the only) way is through metaphor. Metaphor does not contradict or devalue the power of cognitive signification. While respecting the results of cognition, it tries other doors. The fable is told in signs but its action differs from cognition's. In this respect, an asymmetry between the two persists. The cognitive sign makes reference to the cognitive realm while metaphor points beyond its. Yet metaphoric and cognitive meaning coexist. We are beings of plural aspects. As to how the plurality is transformed in the moment of self-revelation, only a deeper self-knowing can say.

NOTES

PREFACE

1. Jacques Derrida, *Of Grammatology*, tr. Gayatri Chakravorty Spivak (Baltimore: John Hopkins University Press, 1976) p. 266.

CHAPTER 1

1. Aristotle, in, *The Basic Works of Aristotle*, ed. Richard McKeon (New York: Random House, 1941).

2. Cited in Susan Sontag, *Illness as Metaphor* (New York: Farrar, Straus, and Giroux) p. 34n.

3. Aristotle, in *Basic Works*.

4. Emily Brontë, *Wuthering Heights* (New York: Pocket Books, 1954) p. 198.

5. René Descartes, Meditation II, in Elizabeth Haldane and G.R.T. Ross, *The Philosophical Works of Descartes*, I (Cambridge: Cambridge University Press, 1969) p. 150.

6. John Locke, *An Essay Concerning Human Understanding*, ed. A.S. Pringle-Pattison (Oxford: The Clarendon Press, 1924) p. 223.

7. Plato, *The Collected Dialogues of Plato*, ed. Edith Hamilton and Huntington Cairns (New York: Pantheon, 1961).

8. Thomas Hobbes, in *The English Philosophers from Bacon to Mill*, ed. Edwin Burtt (New York: Random House 1939) p. 141.

9. Locke, p. 231.

10. Ibid., p. 239.

11. Plato, *Dialogues*.

12. René Descartes, in *The Philosophical Works of Descartes*, tr. Elizabeth S. Haldane and G.R.T. Ross (Cambridge: Cambridge University Press, 1969) p. 84.

13. Jean-Jacques Rousseau, "Essay On the Origin of Languages," in *On the Origin of Language*, tr. John H. Moran and Alexander Gode (New York: F. Ungar Publishing Co., 1966) p. 49.

14. Ibid., p. 291.

15. Ibid., p. 293; italics added.

CHAPTER 2

1. Descartes, in Haldane and Ross, p. 385.

2. Baruch Spinoza, *The Ethics*, Part IV, proposition xlii, tr. R.H.M. Elwes (New York: Dover, 1955) p. 217.

3. Richard Wilhelm, tr., *The I Ching* (Princeton: Princeton University Press, 1950) p. 197.

4. Herman Melville, *Moby Dick* (New York: Platt & Munk, 1964) p. 127.

5. T.S. Eliot, "Burnt Norton," in *The Complete Poems and Plays* (New York: Harcourt, Brace & World, 1952) p. 118.

6. Frederich Nietzsche, "Thus Spoke Zarathustra," in *The Portable Nietzsche*, vol. 3, tr. Walter Kaufmann (New York: The Viking Press, 1954) p. 275.

7. Jean-Jacques Rousseau, "A Discourse on the Origin of Inequality," in *The Social Contract* and *Discourses*, tr. G.D.H. Cole (London: J.M. Dent & Sons, 1913) p. 176.

8. Frederich Nietzsche, *The Gay Science*, tr. Walter Kaufmann (New York: Random House, 1974) pp. 347-348.

9. Locke, p. 240.

10. Tr. Thomas and J.C. Cleary, *The Blue Cliff Record* (Boulder, CO: Shambala, 1977) II, p. 429.

11. Fyodor Dostoyevsky, *The Brothers Karamazov*, tr. Constance Garnett (New York: Random House, 1950) p. 122.

12. Hobbes, p. 153.

13. Arthur Schopenhauer, *The World as Will and Representation*, tr. E.F.J. Payne (New York: Dover, 1958) II, p. 91.

14. Descartes, in Haldane and Ross, p. 386.

15. Aristotle, *Basic Works*.

16. Baruch Spinoza, "Tractaus Politicus," in *Works of Spinoza*, tr. R.H.M. Elwes (New York: Dover, 1955) I, sec. 4.

17. Emily Brontë, *Wuthering Heights* (New York: Pocket Books, 1954) p. 250.

18. Plato, *Dialogues*.

19. Locke, pp. 231-232.

20. Edmund Husserl, *Logical Investigations*, tr. J.N. Findlay (New York: Humanities Press, 1970) I, sec. 7, p. 277.

21. Ibid., sec. 8, p. 279.

22. Ibid., p. 275.

CHAPTER 3

1. Martin Heidegger, *The Question Concerning Technology*, tr. William Lovitt, (New York: Harper & Row, 1977) p. 13.

2. Hobbes, p. 140.

3. Descartes, in Haldane and Ross, p. 146.

4. Descartes, in Haldane and Ross, p. 340.

5. Ibid., p. 351.

6. Descartes in Haldane and Ross, II, pp. 103-104.

7. René Descartes, *Oeuvres de Descartes*, ed. Charles Adam and P. Tannery (Paris: Vrin, 1897-1910) IV, p. 573; trans. Norman Kemp Smith, *New Studies in the Philosophy of Descartes* (New York: Russell & Russell, 1963) pp. 134-135.

8. Ibid., III, p. 148.

CHAPTER 4

1. Thomas Hobbes, pp. 140-141.

2. Ibid., p. 141.

3. Ibid., p. 143.

4. Ibid., p. 142.

5. Ibid., p. 162.

6. Ferdinand de Saussure, *Course in General Linguistics*, tr. Wade Baskin (New York: Philosophical Library, 1959) pp. 118-119.

7. Ibid., p. 120.

8. Ibid., p. 10.

9. David Hume, *A Treatise of Human Nature*, ed. L.A. Selby-Bigge (Oxford: The Clarendon Press, 1888) I.I.3, p. 8.

10. Saussure, pp. 13, 15.

11. Ibid., p. 15.

12. Hobbes, p. 202.

13. Ibid., p. 173.

14. Ibid., p. 198.

15. Ibid., p. 163.

16. Ibid., p. 141.

17. Michel Foucault, *Madness and Civilization*, tr. Richard Howard (New York: Pantheon, 1965) p. 74.

18. Hobbes, pp. 143-144.

19. Ibid., p. 147.

20. Ibid., p. 197.

21. Ibid., p. 208.

22. Ibid., p. 162.

23. Ibid., p. 161.

CHAPTER 5

1. Hobbes, *Leviathan*, p. 148.

2. Ibid., p. 129.

3. Ibid., p. 152.

4. Ibid., p. 153.

5. Ibid., p. 133.

6. Ibid., p. 133.

7. Ibid., p. 133.

8. Ibid., p. 153.

9. Ibid., p. 152.

10. Ibid., p. 133.

11. Ibid., p. 134.

12. Ibid., p. 148.

13. Ibid., p. 153.

14. Ibid., p. 133.

15. Ibid., p. 145.

16. Ibid., p. 142.

17. Ibid., p. 147.

18. Ibid., p. 147.

19. Ibid., p. 141.

20. Ibid., p. 133.

21. Ibid., p. 138.

22. Ibid., p. 146.

23. Ibid., p. 141.

Chapter 6

1. Jean-Jacques Rousseau, *Emile*, tr. Barbara Foxley (London: J.M. Dent and Sons, 1911) p. 32.

2. M.M. Lewis, *Infant Speech* (London: Kegan Paul, 1951).

3. Rousseau, *Essay*, p. 176.

4. Roman Jakobson, *Child Language, Aphasia, and Phonological Universals* (The Hague: Mouton, 1968) p. 24.

5. Ibid., p. 25.

6. Ibid., p. 28.

7. Ibid., p. 25.

8. Etienne Bonnot de Condillac, *An Essay on the Origin of Human Knowledge,* tr. Thomas Nugent (Gainesville, FL: Scholars' Facsimiles & Reprints, 1971) p. 172.

9. Ibid., p. 179.

10. Ibid., p. 174.

11. Ibid., p. 181.

12. *Logic*, in *Philosophical Writings of Etienne Bonnot, Abbé de Condillac*, tr. Franklin Philip (Hillsdale, NJ: Lawrence Erlbaum Associates, 1982) II.2, p. 389.

13. *Essay*, p. 180.

14. Ibid., p. 180.

15. Ibid., p. 174.

16. Ibid., p. 228.

17. Ibid., p. 273.

18. Ibid., p. 283.

19. Ibid., p. 178.

20. Ibid., p. 178.

21. Ibid., p. 18.

CHAPTER 7

1. Maurice Merleau-Ponty, *Phenomenology of Perception*, tr. Colin Smith (New York: The Humanities Press, 1962) p. 187.

2. Ibid., pp. 187-188.

3. Ibid., p. 188.

4. Ibid., p. 189.

5. Ibid., p. 189.

6. Ibid., p. 194.

7. Ibid.

8. Herbert Spencer, "On the Origin and Function of Music," *Essays on Education and Kindred Subjects*, ed. Charles W. Eliot (New York: Dent, 1910) pp. 320-321.

9. Condillac, *Essay*, p. 182.

10. Ibid., p. 181.

11. Ibid., p. 181.

12. Ibid., p. 180.

13. Ibid., pp. 180-181.

14. Ibid., p. 182.

15. Ibid., p. 182.

16. Ibid., pp. 183-184.

17. Ibid., p. 184.

18. Ibid., p. 184.

19. Ibid., p. 184.

20. Ibid., p. 185.

21. Ibid., pp. 193-194.

22. Ibid., p. 195.

23. Ibid., p. 182.

24. Ibid., p. 196.

25. Ibid., p. 197.

26. Ibid., pp. 197-198.

27. Ibid., pp. 200-201.

28. Ibid., p. 212.

29. Ibid., p. 223.

30. Ibid., p. 223.

31. Ibid., p. 225.

CHAPTER 8

1. Wilhelm von Humboldt, *Linguistic Variability and Intellectual Development*, tr. George C. Buck and Frithjof A. Raven (Coral Gables, FL: University of Miami Press, 1971).

2. Ludwig Wittgenstein, *Philosophical Investigations*, tr. G.E.M. Anscombe (Oxford: Basil Blackwell, 1963) 338, p. 109.

3. Ibid., II, xi, p. 208.

4. D.L. Omsted, *Out of the Mouth of Babes* (The Hague: Mouton, 1971) p. 35.

5. See D.B. Fry, "The development of the phonological system in the normal and the deaf child," in F. Smith and G.A. Miller eds., *The Genesis of Language* (Cambridge: M.I.T. Press, 1966).

6. Jakobson, p. 42.

7. Ibid., p. 24.

8. Ibid., p. 25.

9. Ibid., p. 29.

10. Ibid., p. 27.

11. Ibid., p. 22.

12. Condillac, *Writings*, pp. 330-331.

13. Jakobson, p. 25.

14. Condillac, *Writings*, p. 331.

15. Pierre Marie, *Travaux et Memoires*, I; *L'aphasie* (Paris: 1926); cited in Jakobson, p. 38.

16. Jakobson, p. 36.

17. Condillac, *Writings*, p. 331.

18. Ibid., p. 331.

19. Ibid., p. 331.

20. Hobbes, p. 137.

21. William James, *The Principles of Psychology*, I (New York: Dover, 1950) p. 416.

22. Condillac, *Writings*, p. 332.

23. James, p. 266.

24. Cited in James, p. 267.

25. Wittgenstein, 342, pp. 109-110.

26. Condillac, *Essay*, p. 173.

27. Ibid., p. 174.

28. Cited in MacDonald Critchley, *Silent Language* (London: Butterworths, 1975) p. 55.

29. Denis Diderot, "Letter on the Deaf and Dumb," in *Diderot's Early Philosophical Works*, tr. Margaret Jourdain (Chicago: Open Court, 1916) p. 187.

30. Ibid., p. 187.

31. Ibid., p. 187.

CHAPTER 9

Epigraph to this chapter: Denis Diderot, *Lettres à Sophie Volland*, ed. A. Babelon (Paris: Gallimard, 1938) II, pp. 233-234.

1. Herman Melville, *Moby Dick*, p. 363.

2. Condillac, *Essay*, p. 229.

3. Ibid., p. 229.

4. Ibid., p. 229.

5. Ibid., p. 234.

6. Ibid., p. 231.

7. Ibid., p. 232.

8. Ibid., p. 227.

9. Ibid., p. 279.

10. Ibid., p. 237.

11. Ibid., pp. 237-238.

12. Ibid., p. 228.

13. Ibid., p. 236.

14. Ibid., p. 236.

15. Denis Diderot, *Oeuvres completes*, ed. Assezat-Tourneux (Nendelu, Liechtenstein: Kraus, 1966) XI, p. 134. Subsequent references to volume and page are from this edition.

16. Denis Diderot, *Correspondance*, ed. G. Roth (Paris: Editions de Minuit, 1955-1970) Subsequent references to Diderot's correspondence will be to this edition.

CHAPTER 10

1. Plato, *Republic*, in, *The Collected Dialogues of Plato*, ed. Edith Hamilton and Huntington Cairns (New York: Pantheon, 1961). All subsequent references to the works of Plato are from this edition.

2. Sophocles, "Oedipus Rex," tr. R.C. Jebb, in *The Complete Greek Drama* I, ed. Whitney J. Oates and Eugene O'Neill, Jr. (New York: Random House, 1938) 1385-1398.

3. Hobbes, p. 141.

4. Cited at *Republic* 390d.

PARTIAL BIBLIOGRAPHY

Aristotle. *The Basic Works of Aristotle.* Ed. Richard McKeon. New York: Random House, 1941.

——. *The Works of Aristotle.* Vol. 3-6. Ed. J.A. Smith and W.D. Ross. Oxford: The Clarendon Press, 1911-1914.

Condillac, Etienne Bonnot de. *An Essay on the Origin of Human Knowledge.* Tr. Thomas Nugent. Gainesville, FL: Scholars' Facsimilies & Reprints, 1971.

——. *Philosophical Writings of Etienne Bonnot, Abbé de Condillac.* Tr. Franklin Philip. Hillsdale, NJ: Lawrence Erlbaum Associates, 1982.

Cruttenden, Alan. *Language in Infancy and Childhood.* New York: St. Martin's Press, 1979.

Derrida, Jacques. *Of Grammatology.* Tr. Gayatri Chakravorty Spivak. Baltimore: Johns Hopkins University Press, 1976.

——. *Speech and Phenomena.* Tr. David Allison. Evanston, IL: Northwestern University Press, 1973.

Descartes, René. *The Philosophical Works of Descartes.* Tr. Elizabeth S. Haldane and G.R.T. Ross. Cambridge: Cambridge University Press, 1969.

Diderot, Denis. *Diderot's Early Philosophical Works.* Tr. Margaret Jourdain. Chicago: Open Court, 1916.

——. *Oeuvres completes.* Ed. J. Assezat and M. Tourneux. Nendeln, Liechtenstin: Kraus, 1966.

Haldane, Elizabeth S., and Ross, G.R.T., tr. *The Philosophical Works of Descartes.* Cambridge: Cambridge University Press, 1969.

Hobbes, Thomas. "Leviathan." In *The English Philosophers from Bacon to Mill*. Ed. Edwin A. Burtt. New York: Random House, 1939.

Husserl, Edmund. *Logical Investigations*. Tr. J.N. Findlay. New York: Humanities Press, 1970.

Jakobson, Roman. *Child Language, Aphasia, and Phonological Universals*. The Hague: Mouton, 1968.

James, William. *The Principles of Psychology*. Vol. 1. New York: Dover, 1950.

Locke, John. *An Essay Concerning Human Understanding*. Ed. A.S. Pringle-Pattison. Oxford: The Clarendon Press, 1924.

Malmberg, Bertil. *Phonetics*. New York: Dover, 1963.

Merleau-Ponty, Maurice. *Consciousness and the Acquisition of Language*. Tr. Hugh Silverman. Evanston, IL: Northwestern University Press, 1973.

——— . *Phenomenology of Perception*. Tr. Colin Smith. London: Routledge, 1962.

Olmsted, D.L. *Out of the Mouth of Babes*. The Hague: Mouton, 1971.

Plato. *The Collected Dialogues of Plato*. Ed. Edith Hamilton and Huntington Cairns. New York: Pantheon, 1961.

Perkins, William H., and Kent, Raymond D. *Functional Anatomy of Speech, Language, and Hearing*. San Diego, CA: College-Hill Press, 1986.

Rousseau, Jean Jacques. *Emile*. Tr. Barbara Foxley. London: J.M. Dent & Sons, 1911.

——— . In *The Social Contract* and *Discourses*. Tr. G.D.H. Cole. London: J.M. Dent & Sons, 1913.

——— . In *Essay on the Origin of Language*. In, *On the Origin of Language*, Tr. John H. Moran and Alexander Gode. New York: F. Ungar Pub. Co., 1966.

Saussure, Ferdinand de. *Course in General Linguistics*. Tr. Wade Baskin. New York: Philosophical Library, 1959.

Wittgenstein, Ludwig. *Philosophical Investigations*. Tr. G.E.M. Anscombe, Oxford: Basil Blackwell, 1963.

INDEX